3, rue Beautreillis
75004 Paris
ISBN 2-906571-25-3

FRANÇOIS DAGOGNET

IN FAVOUR OF TODAY'S ART

From the Object of Art to the Art of the Object

Translated from the French by
MARINA PALMER
PATRICK WOTLING

THIS SERIES EDITED BY DANIELE RIVIERE

IN THE SAME SERIES

SOUND AND THE VISUAL ARTS, *Intersections between Music and Plastic Arts today,*
edited by Jean-Yves Bosseur

FOREWORD

Though a University professor specialized in the history of sciences and techniques, as well as a philosopher, I intend to concentrate on art,—looking at it mainly from the angle of its historical development. My concern with machines and tools, which at first may appear to be a limiting factor, should not in fact be too much of a handicap.

For a long time, the relationship between art on the one hand and on the other industry (considered as prosaic, inhuman and fundamentally hostile to any form of culture) was one of conflict. So romanticism turned away from the mechanical world, extolled that of nature and the manual work of the craftsman who lends an individual stamp to his creation, a privilege inaccessible to the factory-worker. Then decorative art widened the gap (the School of Ruskin, just as the French School of Nancy was to do later on), in spite of severe criticism (Giedion, Benjamin).

Since then however, art has progressively taken on the values of the factory, advertising, architecture, electronics, as well as numerous synthetic materials (first and foremost plastics, then aluminium, chromium, cold-rolled steel, and sometimes new types of glass). Today's designer, like the engineer, merely lays out a plan: he programs the object which he then leaves to a skilful craftsman to produce. Manual work is no more part of the creative process[1]. As a result and testifying to a major change, the creative process has lost its aura: it no longer aims to give rise to a unique object, but from the start claims to produce objects in series (multiple objects), thus paralleling the mass-production of goods.

(1) — Except in the work of some minimalist or conceptual artists such as Artschwager, for instance.

Given my personal inclinations with all they imply, I am perfectly aware that my approach may be partial or even inadequate; I nevertheless believe it to be a better one than that of some interpreters (whom I will criticize along the way), bogged down in their scholarly historical concerns or blinded by mere results, and who grossly ignore means, materials and processes.

It is not the first time that I have placed great emphasis on the comparison between the artist and the scientist (physics and chemistry generally): whereas the latter's aim is to discover relationships or even laws governing phenomena, the former on the contrary—less interested in relationships than in substrata—seeks to grasp matter by exploring its breath-taking and unfathomable qualities (an exercise in sense-perception). What a privilege it is for one to gain an insight into what is usually ignored, the grain, the texture of things!

Let us not restrict ourselves to what is generally considered art; a chapter has been devoted to one of its branches, namely the aesthetics of consumption. This deals with the design of a vase or of a chair. Indeed, an armchair or a lamp is never viewed as fulfilling a merely functional purpose (the imaginary process fortunately comes to prevail and tends to counterbalance the dryness resulting from pure functionalism).

It would have been possible to pursue this still further and to look at what is considered a lower form of art according to the authorized hierarchy—namely poster art (Savignac, Villemot, Excofion), visual advertising, logo.

"But is this still art?", purists will ask. My reply is that renowned artists such as Toulouse-Lautrec, Delaunay or Magritte willingly worked in this field which has been wrongly despised.

Novelists and poets themselves point us in that direction, Francis Ponge in particular. He felt that literature had been invaded and poisoned by anthropology so that he devoted his work to the "parti pris des choses.[2]" No one has invited us so eagerly as he to discover the world of objects—be it a pebble, a glass of water, a lump of earth, even mud, floorboards or an ash-tray. "Our aim is for the object gradually to impose all

(2) — The author refers to the title of one of Francis Ponge's famous works. This title is a pun meaning both "taking sides with things" or "in defence of things", and "the prejudice of things", emphasizing the fact that they are never neutral. (Translators' note).

or at least some of its qualities on us, however different they may be from those commonly associated with it. It is for us never to yield to an arrangement of qualities which seems harmonious [...] One really must integrate a quality even if it is demeaning or anti-poetical [...] One must not organize things [...] Things must be disturbing. They must force us out of our routine; there is nothing so worthwhile, for there is nothing else which helps the mind to progress.[3]"

Thanks to Ponge, a problem is solved: "If somebody says to me—and people have often reproached me for it: man is of no interest to you, I smile. They are quite right, I am fed up with man the way he is, I am fed up with this game. Let us get out of this, we must let our objects save us from this... What more revolutionary thing than an object? What greater bomb than this cigarette-butt, than this ash-tray?"[4]

The present text—the purpose of which is to make us aware of the development of art, as well as of the existence of what I have called "domo-aesthetics"—ends with a reply to the following objection: is it not a mistake to take the spoon or the armchair seriously? On the contrary, I believe the reverse to be true. Art has confined itself too strictly to man and his artful creation; it has withdrawn too completely from everyday life. The humblest as well as the most utilitarian object allows us to return to it in that it pulls down the barriers that closed off and limited the cultural field. It puts an end to former divisions. Modern and contemporary art abolishes the oldest partitions.

The path I have chosen does not lead to a conservative attitude, nor into a maze of trinkets and trivialities, in my opinion. And in conclusion, it is my belief that in the humblest materiality as well as in the most elementary organization, the purest art may glitter.

(3) — Francis Ponge, *Méthodes*, Idées/Gallimard, Paris, 1961, pp. 262-263.
(4) — Id., p. 266.

«It has always been my contention that a picture is not a representation of things, but that it is a thing."

Antoni Tapiès, *l'Art contre l'Esthétique,*
Galilée, Paris, 1974, p. 167

"If I had called what I do painting, people would have told me that it is sculpture, and if I had called it sculpture, they would have told me that it is bas-relief or painting."

Robert Rauschenberg, *l'Aventure de l'Art au XXe siècle,*
edited by J.-L. Ferrier, Chêne-Hachette, Paris, 1988, p. 609

CHAPTER I

Towards the recognition and the understanding of the object

My first concern is the object and I propose to define it—and above all to rescue it—by dismissing any observations which might not do credit to it. If it is, as I believe, to play a greater role in today's art field, it would be proper to allow it to do so: maintaining the old—and sometimes century-old—prejudices which weigh it down makes the magnificent promotion it deserves impossible.

Modern and contemporary art calls forth the object just as the flower calls forth the fruit; yet, in order for the artistic process to reach its total fulfilment, the reverse must also be true: in its turn, the humblest, the most banal object calls forth a style which is able to transform it (design). But how can a casserole, a pan or an electric lamp be "artistic"? The situation is unsettling, to say the least.

The visual arts are not the only ones to be touched by this development; literature too has been affected, Alain Robbe-Grillet and Francis Ponge, among others, bear witness to this. But first, it is necessary to clear the ground: what is an object in itself?, we may ask, and why does it deserve our attention?

***

In spite of what Duchamp may have said, the object undoubtedly is that which has been or is in the process of being shaped by a subject. The spotlight has always been on the demiurge whereas the result of his operation has always been left in the dark. How can one explain this tendency? From the start, culture has always leaned in this direction: it minimizes the importance of the "deposit" or of materiality, concentrating on the origin rather than on the result; the emphasis is placed on the command rather than on the execution.

It should be noted here that the object is not identical to its image (or its double) because the latter implies the exhaustive reproduction of the former. The object is also kept at a distance or removed and, which is more, it loses its three-dimensional materiality. It is very easy to follow this intellectualist or idealistic inclination. The subject could have shaped some other product, we think, and this makes this one appear relative or random. All sorts of converging factors tend to privilege one of the terms—the origin, that which is indispensable—and to underestimate the other—the effect. Inevitably, the cause is given greater importance than the consequence.

However, the reverse opinion could (or should) have come to prevail, for it is in the objects shaped by man themselves that the inventive devices are located, the successful execution of which can only be measured in the tangible product, for the purely spiritual element is nothing in itself. An idea must be embodied to be recognized and analysed. So there is nothing so worthwhile as the actualization, the concrete realization of a plan: instead of forgetting or underrating this process, we should consider it the witness and the real guardian of thought. Everyone knows Mallarmé's phrase, on which Valéry commented: "It is neither with feelings nor with ideas that a poem is written, but with words, in and through the sole process of writing."

Let us proceed somewhat farther: civilizations express themselves more genuinely through their tools, and the medley of instruments of everyday use, than through their thoughts (which are vague and therefore difficult to know). But the proliferation and the richness of these objects prevent us from really understanding them: as a result, they make up a world of unusual and queer things, which we call "curiosities." Glancing at a second-hand shop-window, or wandering through a flea-market is enough to make us feel stunned. It is easy to lose contact with what one sees, for objects to appear strange, especially when they are piled together. As a result, pejorative terms such as "jumble," "bric-à-brac" and "odds and ends" are often used when referring to them. But the only real reason for these unfair names is ignorance.

Let us inquire into the real causes of this attitude, which is very close to hostility. Criticism was bred and encouraged by the so-called consumption-society, saturated with goods, and believed by thinkers to be the utmost degree of alienation and uniformization because, according to them, every individual is completely drowned in the world of goods. However, it is in the interest of these detractors—who are themselves in possession of what they disparage—to advocate these ideas: do not aim at ownership, they seem to insinuate, this would corrupt your mind and lead to your downfall. The rich discourage the desire for things; they speak in praise of deprivation with much talent: according to them, we should content ourselves with what is easily available to everyone. But is this not the symptom that their appetites are more than satisfied? Have these same people not already acquired what they consider futile and dangerous at the same time? What greater hypocrisy than the "moralizing" attitude?

Why have philosophers so readily recommended asceticism? Why have they written in praise of poverty and even of self-sacrifice? Back in time, what explanation for Diogenes and his barrel? Why should wisdom necessarily imply renouncement, and the sacrifice of anything but that which is strictly necessary—when it is precisely all that is cumbersome, superfluous and ruinous for which one longs? Why use a glass or a cup when one could easily get water directly from the spring and drink it straight out of one's hands? It is certainly true that the desire to possess things can lead to a form of neurosis (appropriation-neurotics), so that a warning is justifiable: the collector's aim is to own "unique pieces" of which the others are deprived, and which they cannot boast to possess. Undoubtedly, this is a display of power (sadism), but let us not confuse a mere function with its pathological deviance. No one would ever dream of attacking knowledge in itself because of a similar neurosis to which it may give rise, namely obsessional erudition (another example of retention).

But from the start, Plato guided thought in this direction: he moralizes and praises poverty. Only metics are allowed to produce, manage and sell merchandise (just as, in the Middle-Ages, the professions implying direct contact with money were restricted to the persecuted Jews). Plato even insists on that his "ideal City" should be placed far from the coast or from rivers, far from their harbours and their warehouses: "If it were going to be founded near the sea and have good harbours," he writes in *The Laws*, "[...] then a very great saviour indeed and lawgivers of divine stature would be needed to stop sophisticated and vicious characters developing on a grand scale: such a state would simply invite it.[1]" Plato seeks to reduce the trade and manufacture of goods to a minimum: no member of the City is allowed to live by lucrative manual labour, restricted to foreigners, and strictly limited to certain days, at certain hours, and in certain places.

In *The Republic*, he already divides society into three groups. The craftsman, the shopkeeper and the ploughman are at the bottom of the pyramid. In the middle is the soldier, whose selflessness is the result of the sharing of women, children and goods (guaranteeing him against greed) and of his loyalty, given that he is prepared to die for his city. At the top is the philosopher-legislator, whose task is to organize the whole of the City (the concrete universal). One gradually moves away from needs and the necessity to satisfy them, from desire, possession, and from the body generally. One must detach oneself from the world of the senses. Plato's social classification still lives on in the western civilization: for centuries, the priest and the soldier have continued to be considered nobler than the ploughman and those who do practical work in general.

The Cynics followed and came down even more strongly on manual work; they too preached a form of detachment: "Having seen a young child drinking out of his hands, Diogenes took his cup from his bag and threw it away, saying: 'A young child is ahead of me on the path of frugality'. So, he threw his bowl away too.[2]" The message is to free ourselves from that which invades our lives. Diogenes shows us how to go about it, taking it to the limit. All he needs is a cloak (the tribon), be it winter or summer, day or night: "He was easily able to stay in the open air out of habit. He never covered his feet, saying that they are no more sensitive than the eyes, or than the face. Although they are more vulnerable by nature, these parts of the body can easily stand the cold when they are constantly exposed. Indeed, people do not walk with their eyes covered, as they do with their feet. He (Diogenes) used to say that the rich are like new-born children. For they are all wrapped up in swaddling clothes.[3]"

(1) — *The Laws*, 704 d, translated by Trevor J. Saunders, Penguin Books, Harmondsworth, 1970, p. 159.
(2) — *L'ascèse cynique*, Marie-Odile Goulet-Cazé, Vrin, Paris, 1986, p. 58.

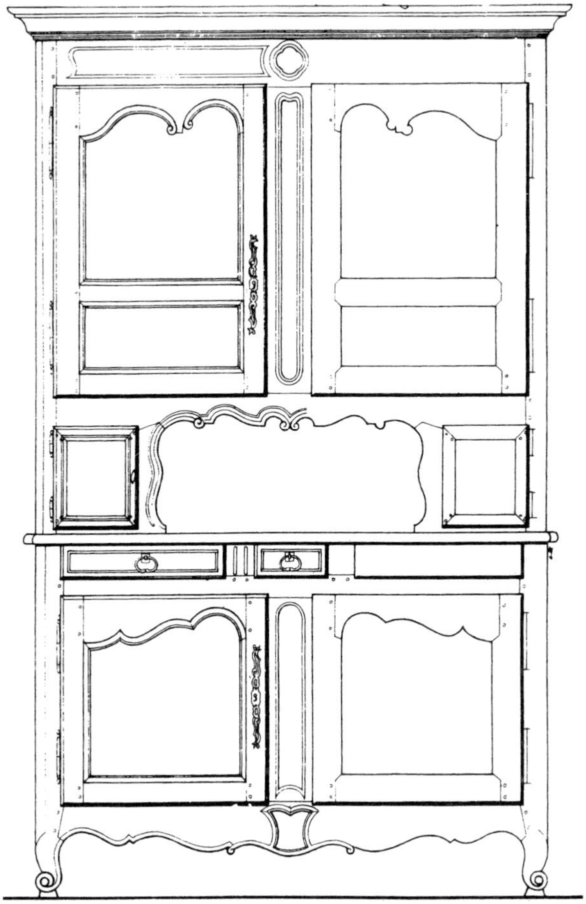

1 – Unity and discontinuity. The duality of the inside and the outside

Off with sandals, covers and wrappings! Of what use are they?

Diogenes goes even further: he strives to imitate animals, and aims to behave like the dogs in the streets (hence the word "cynicism," from the greek *kuôn*, *kunos*, dog); he eats raw flesh, for instance. "Diogenes used to mock those who walk past springs without stopping when they are thirsty, in order to find at all costs Chio or Lesbos wine. They are less reasonable than the animals in the fields, he would say. For they, at least, never go past a spring or a stream of pure water without stopping when they are thirsty.[4]" Animals are characterized by their health, their strength, their balance. What is their secret? Diogenes' answer is: "They own nothing.[5]"

Why does one go to such lengths to defend extreme poverty? Our objects are linked to three basic functions, all of them related to the body: nourishment, clothing and housing. Diogenes shows that we have very few needs since nature has seen to our maintenance. Hence his recommendation of abstinence, and his own restriction to the cloak as blanket at night, and tunic during the day (his other belongings being a pouch, and finally a barrel). The philosopher's goal is independence and self-control. In my opinion, however, it is a lie. For on the one hand, the wise man's aspiration towards virtue through asceticism is possible only because he has cleverly left all business and labour to the less privileged; his only concern is to carve out his own singularity and superiority. Just as machines were unnecessary in the days of slavery, as is well known, so too, it is unnecessary for the thinker to occupy himself with that which is done by the pedlar, the shopkeeper and the craftsman. On the other hand, and more importantly, an ostentatious display of self-control is necessary if one is to rule others; in this way, one consolidates one's "elitist outlook" and one's superiority.

And finally, renouncement can be seen in terms of a ritual initiation. For the act of renouncement is rarely merely a sign of temperance: it gives rise mainly to the recognition of a power (be it moral, social, economic, political). What stronger power—and yet what more dangerous? For he who masters his own body believes that he has the right to direct the souls of others.

(3) — Id., p. 59.
(4) — Id., p. 64.
(5) — Id., p. 65.

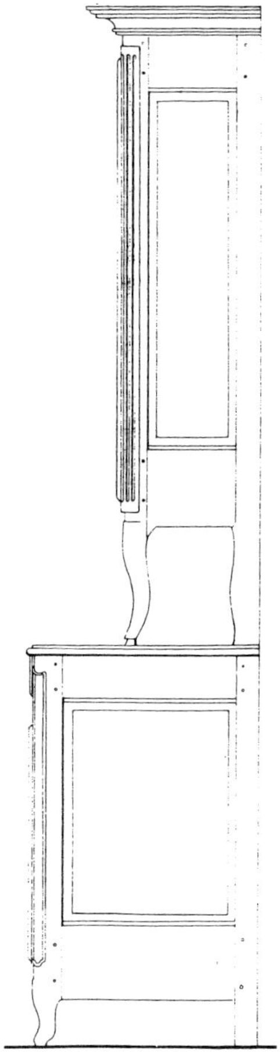

2 – The upper body may stand on the lower one

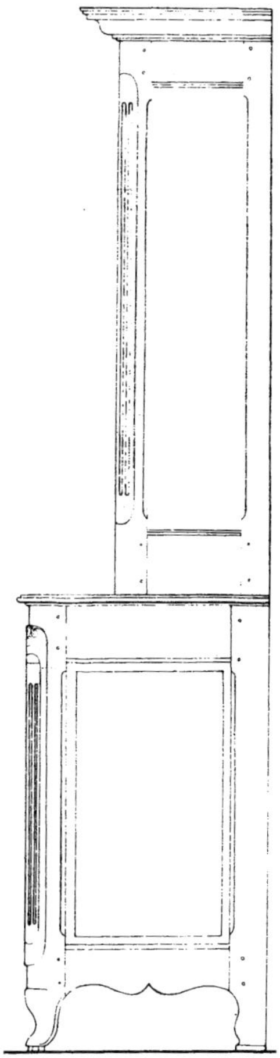

3 – A continuous arrangement of the two bodies

Today however, the strongest and most legitimate criticism against the world of products is not any longer inspired by the values of ancient aristocracy; it bases its charge upon the evils committed by our industrial civilization and its inherent flaws—and this is the only complaint to be heard.

a) The argument goes: the economic process can be divided into four stages, all closely linked and interdependent: design, machine-production, distribution and consumption. Now, the second stage, namely the apparatus of production, has become so predominant that it determines the other stages, that is the nature of the goods as well as their distribution and sale. As a result, a kind of totalitarianism has emerged, overwhelming the powerless individual. Manufactured goods cannot be put on the market without the help of advertising—a form of dictatorship which finally gives rise to "artificial needs," and thus increases the alienation of the subjects.

So, thinkers rightly warn us against this double bondage: they praise moderation as well as peaceful and natural pleasures. We are back to the glass of water, to fresh air, to an unpolluted earth.

b) Moreover, one of the main features of the manufacturing system is the inevitable waste it involves, as well as all sorts of destructive consequences. Disorder is always the result of a discrepancy: whereas machines produce more and more, factory workers either cannot afford to buy what they manufacture, or else, they rush on cheap goods. In short, the market becomes unbalanced.

Be that as it may, Herbert Marcuse writes: "[...] if the worker and his boss enjoy the same television program and visit the same resort places, if the typist is as attractively made up as the daughter of her employer, if the negro owns a Cadillac, if they all read the same newspaper, then this assimilation indicates not the disappearance of classes, but the extent to which the needs and satisfactions that serve the preservation of the Establishment are shared by the underlying population.[6]"

The manufacturing system is not only alienating—it has become a real trap: by wanting to acquire those products which it cleverly puts on the market, one accepts and perpetuates the whole system which is exploiting

(6) — H. Marcuse, *One-dimensional Man, Studies in the Ideology of Advanced Industrial Society*, Beacon Press, Boston, 1964, p. 8.

one. One is both assimilating it and being assimilated by it. Is it possible, under such circumstances, to defend those "objects" which contribute so effectively to such manipulation?

One should not confuse the issue however. Far from defending the way in which the market is presently organized, I only wish to query whether the effect—namely the desire for abundance—and the cause should be linked, and whether it would not be possible to maintain the former without submitting to the latter.

Besides, those critics have nothing to propound but hatred for machines. Yet, are we not all aware of the violent and murderous nature of the rousseauist myth, that of the return to an original state?

Not very long ago, Henri Bergson told the same old story: "We reproach it (civilization) with having too strongly encouraged artificial ones (needs), with having fostered luxury, with having favoured the towns to the detriment of the countryside, lastly with having widened the gap and revolutionized the relations between employer and employed, between capital and labour.[7]" Hence a host of recommendations: frugality, the refusal of all that is considered useless (luxury), the appeal for mysticism in order to counterbalance "mechanics," and so on.

Solutions have not varied much throughout the ages: the "simple life" has always been considered the adequate remedy. Not one of these thinkers, however, has ever explained of what this kind of life consists, nor exactly what these "artificial needs" are. What luxury do they consider to be blameful?

This condemnation is all the less legitimate, in my opinion, as the craftsman's ingeniousness can only be embodied in the goods he produces: it is meaningless to try to give greater status to the subject by deprecating the object since the two are inseparable. One reaches the highest stage of development and a superior status thanks to the other.

A civilization is certainly characterized by its rites and its beliefs, but even more so by the material equipment it makes use of (furniture, kitchen appliances, televisions, videos, hi-fi systems, etc.). I propose to define the object as the embodiment of multiple values, as the expression of the human activity of which it is an extension, and to which it is dedicated.

(7) — Henri Bergson, *The Two Sources of Morality and Religion*, Henry Holt and Company, New York, 1935, p. 296.

The object cannot be separated from its inventor, nor from those who have perfected it, nor from those who have handled it: it constitutes a complex network of anthropological concerns. I wish to emphasize this point for, as will be shown later, the object is allowed to enter into the field of art—and does so triumphantly—only once art has given up mere illusionist representation in order to become "presentation," only once it has stopped aiming at producing illusions (figurative art) and starts to present us with the stuff of reality, even if it means showing it to us in its most elementary or ordinary dimension.

It would be wrong to reject or even to underrate the importance of "the glass of water" or of "the pan"; so let us follow instead the footsteps of Francis Ponge, who was to devote to them his most beautiful "proems," as he put it (an expression which mixes prose and poem).

***

It is my opinion that the object should not be separated from the social or from the human spheres (the etymological meaning of object is "what is placed before," thus implying the presence of someone). The object must be considered the external stamp of its owner's personality to the same extent that it bears the mark of the creator who designed and maybe executed it.

Heidegger's comment on Van Gogh's "one and only pair of shoes" should convince us of this: let us forget for the time being that the artist has painted something which is an "accessory" of everyday life. The real status of this pair of shoes is that of a self-portrait; they tell us more about Van Gogh than if he had painted himself, which goes to show that the object reflects its user's personality in its own way.

"From the dark opening of the worn insides of the shoes the toilsome tread of the worker stands forth. In the stiffly solid heaviness of the shoes there is the accumulated tenacity of her slow trudge through the far-spreading and ever-uniform furrows of the field, swept by a raw wind. On the leather there lies the dampness and saturation of the soil. Under the soles there slides the loneliness of the field-path as the evening declines. In the shoes, there vibrates the silent call of the earth,

4 – Mixing up the two mixtures

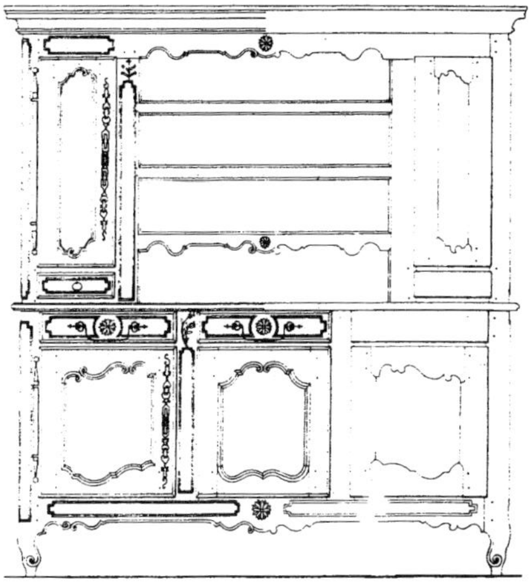

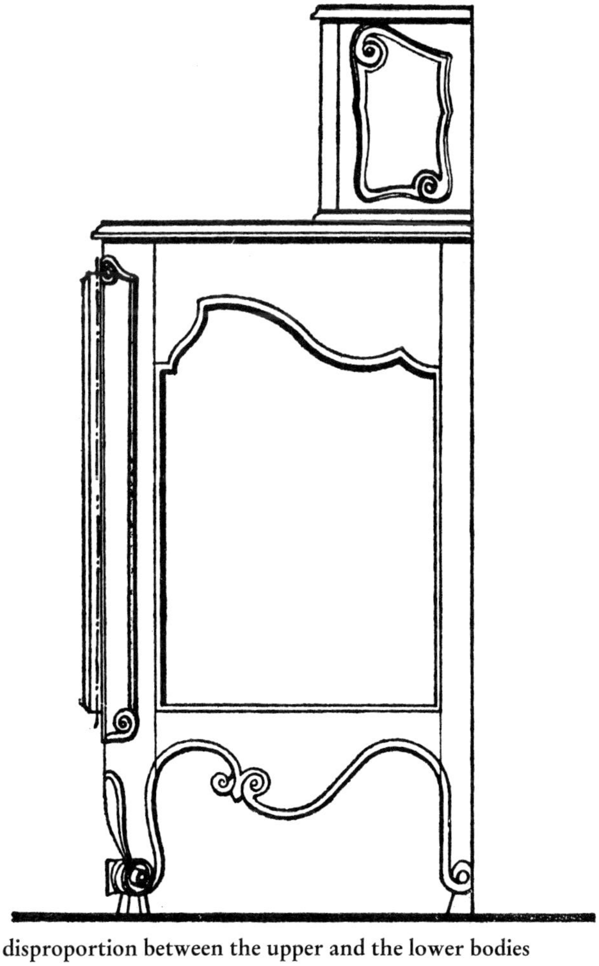

5 – An example of disproportion between the upper and the lower bodies

its quiet gift of the ripening corn and its enigmatic self-refusal in te fallow desolation of the wintry field...[8]"

A contemporary critic, Meyer Schapiro, has discarded this interpretation these are not the shoes of a peasant. These shoes are portrayed in at least eight of Van Gogh's paintings, which leads one to believe that by painting them, he was in fact painting himself. "When Van Gogh depicted the peasant's wooden sabots, he gave them a clear, unworn shape and surface like the smooth still life objects he has set beside them on the same table: the bowl, the bottles, etc. In the later picture of a peasant's leather slippers he has turned them with their backs to the viewer [...]. His own shoes he has isolated on the floor and he has rendered them as if facing us, and so individual and wrinkled in the appearance that we can speak of them as veridical portraits of aging shoes...[9]"

Indeed, they portray in turn the pilgrim, the wanderer, the poor wretch, the vagabond, the tramp—decline and rejection—, depicting thus the man who has worn them, who has taken them off, and who may no longer be with us. "For a painter to represent his worn shoes as the main subject of a picture is for him to express a concern with the fatalities of his social being.[10]"

The boot bears the mark of the ground it has trodden: you cannot find anything more indispensable (an extreme state of things). All in all, I show you that which I could never be deprived of: I might well be buried with my shirt, but my shoes will remain behind, a last testimony to my passage on earth, and to my death.

This analysis allows us to conclude that these boots are not in the least an artistic excuse to develop a poetical art (depicting the soil, the harvest, the sowing period, and the peasant's labour or the path to freedom of escape); but indirectly, they express the wretched state of the poor artist with greater power than if he had painted a self-portrait, confirming that we reveal ourselves through the objects that surround us (our adherences). To take it even further, footmarks on the ground,

(8) — Martin Heidegger, quoted in Meyer Schapiro, "The Still Life as a Personal Object; A Note on Heidegger and Van Gogh", in *The Reach of Mind*, ed. by M. L. Simmel, New York, 1968, p. 204.

(9) — Id., p. 207.

(10) — Id., p. 208.

never mind shoes, would be sufficient to reveal one's personality. Let us not cut off the object from the subject by which it is inhabited! And if one takes into consideration the ingeniousness of the craftsman, the object is transformed into a semi-objective semi-subjective constellation. And therefore, the myth whereby there is such a thing as "interiority" must be discarded: interiority cannot be located anywhere but on the outside, in a set of personal belongings by means of which it may be grasped: in the things we wear, ranging from a pair of shoes to the glasses we may own, to a pipe or a cap, all of which make up the large subsection of the self—even though it may appear to belong to the non-self.

In the same book, and on the same theme, Schapiro places great emphasis on the idea that the "subject-matter" of painting—which will more and more frequently turn out to be an "object," as will be shown —expresses the artist's personality; and given that it is the object precisely which has become the subject-matter of painting, it is fit to express the subject in the most appropriate fashion. How, then, could one set them apart?

Cézanne's apples may be the most striking illustration of this process. It may not be a well-known fact that he "represented" them again and again, in almost all of his pictures.

The apple is in itself a symbol of love and sin (*malum*, in latin, refers both to the apple and to evil).

Although we shall return to the problem of "still-life" later on, we should note from the start that every plastician is characterized by what he chooses to stress or to put forward. "It is hard to conceive of Cézanne painting the epicure Manet's salmon, oysters and asparagus, or Van Gogh's potatoes, sunflowers and shoes.[11]" Moreover, if another artist were to paint apples, necessarily endowed with some sort of symbolic meaning, they would not resemble Cézanne's: no matter how similar the "theme," it would be impossible to mistake them for his apples. Schapiro stresses another characteristic feature: "In studying Chardin's extraordinary *La Raie*, in the Louvre, Cézanne copied from it only the jug and metal pot, but ignored the ray, the cat, the fish, and oysters.[12]" His paintings are devoid of animals. The presence or the absence of

(11) — Meyer Schapiro, "Avant-Garde. The Apples of Cézanne. An Essay on the Meaning of Still Life," in *Selected Papers, Modern Art*, New York, 1977, p. 26.

certain objective elements, as well as the occasional lapses point to a real projection-confession of the artist. In making this remark, Schapiro establishes the ground for a convincing and verifiable aesthetics which has the virtue of doing away with all unfounded speculations.

Cézanne's fruit encloses so many personal dramas that it is almost impossible to decipher. There is no doubt at all that Cézanne uses it as a code. Let us remind ourselves of two pieces of information which might throw some light on the message:

a) a painful recollection: whereas Zola, in *l'Oeuvre*, considers Cézanne a would-be painter, the latter recalls a moving scene from their common childhood: when they were both at school at Aix, Cézanne had shown some sympathy for the young Zola, who was ostracized by his class-mates. Cézanne, who was himself of impulsive and rebelious nature, was given a beating by them because he had spoken to Zola. "The next day, he brought me a large basket of apples.[13]" Thus, an insignificant fruit contains a recollection, a resentment, and a vengeance, all at once.

b) Cézanne's earlier pictures depict either men on the banks of a river without the presence of women, or women without men. It is as if the apple were a way out of this impasse: an imperceptible slide towards forbidden eroticism has been achieved, as well as a struggle against inveterate introversion.

These remarks may seem to have been chosen arbitrarily. And yet, in around 1895, Cézanne declared to "the critic Geffroy [...] that he would astound Paris with an apple" (Paris, Pâris, the name of the character who carried off Helen of Troy). He is also reported to have declared: "I paint still-lifes. Women models frighten me.[14]"

"In paintings of the apples, he was able to express through their more varied colors and groupings a wider range of moods, from the gravely contemplative to the sensual and ecstatic.[15]" The increasing preference shown by Van Gogh or Cézanne for the depiction of shoes on the one hand and apples on the other must undoubtedly be understood in terms of self-depiction. The object should not be seen as being placed *in front of* one, but rather *inside* of and *in relation* to one.

---

(12) — Id., p. 37.
(13) — Id., p. 4.
(14) — Id., p. 30.
(15) — Id., p. 30.

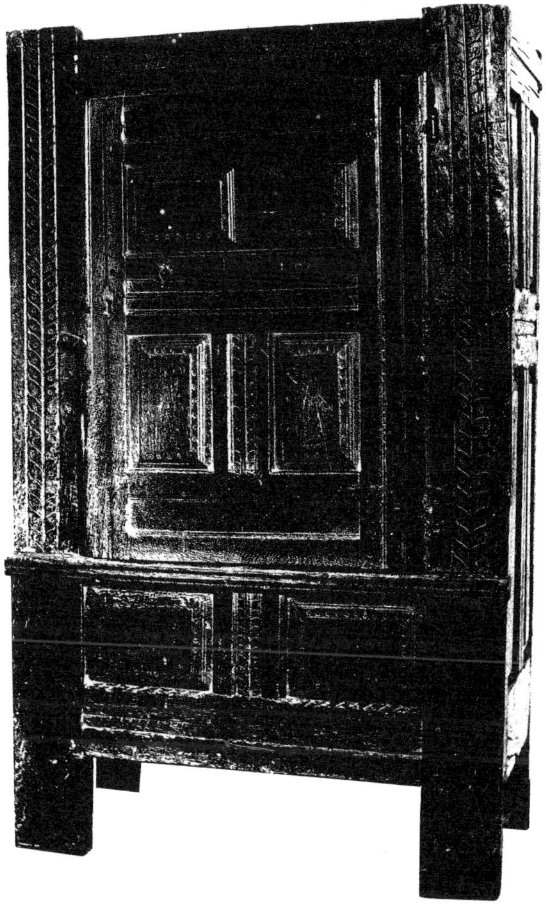

6 – In this case, the upper part is given precedence over the lower one

The same kind of analysis leads to positive results in the field of literature too. A writer's preferences in different areas are visualized with the help of charts: which animals reoccur for instance? Which plants? Which trees, even? Which appliances? Those who have drawn up inventories of this kind have thrown new light on novel- or poetry-writing (it is possible thus to reconstruct prevailing landscapes or scenes which haunt the writer and around which he based the whole narrative). This semantic analysis of a writer's personal vocabulary is highly recommendable. Here at last is an approach to literature in which calculation, counting, and quasi-numerical estimation are not left out! Why choose this particular flower or this particular animal? Why put such emphasis on this particular utensil, and, in the case of transcripts, why omit certain details systematically?

Until now, I have concentrated on privileged objects, or favourite objects. Later, I shall concentrate on those with no subjective emotional significance—objects which have been mechanically built or which have demanded the application of technical skills. Indeed, although it is true to say that the mechanical appliance has little emotional impact, its social and cultural impact remains strong.

Now, it must be stressed that each object—even the most ordinary one (chair, bowl, knife or cupboard) must be approached according to the following criteria:

a) the chosen material; b) the skilful arrangement of pieces or elements, and their organization in the surrounding space; c) the invitation to a certain kind of movement (each chair requires a different position); d) and finally, the originality of the construction, compared with previous models, which have not been merely copied: the whole "structure" has been renewed.

***

In well-documented research papers, anthropologists have frequently insisted on the obvious relation between the most spiritual and exalted feelings on the one hand, and that which weighs them down and carries them, on the other hand: they have recognized the great role played by the material substratum.

In his *Elementary Forms of Religious Life*, for example, Durkheim

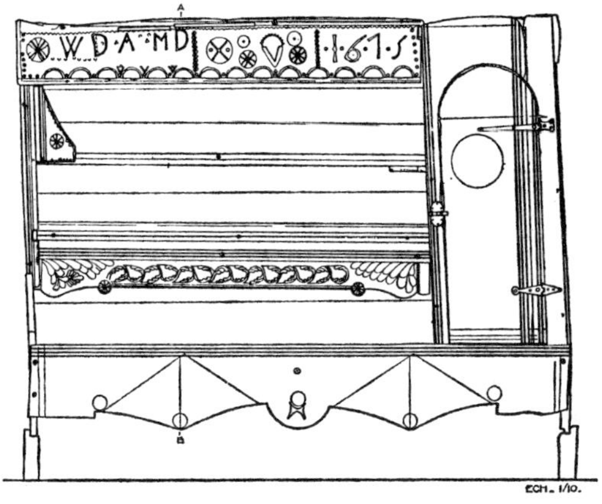

7 – Dissymetry

has shown that the first real religions necessarily included ceremonies, and especially totems, in which the energy or the moral power of society were concentrated, as well as *churinga*, which were ritual instruments treated with great care. The emblem's main function is that of a memory aid—which is why it is reproduced on walls, clothes, weapons, even on bodies (tattoos)—, but it also serves the purpose of rendering concrete the sacred: the life of spirits is thus maintained, making profane life bearable during the time one is cut off from them.

If the totemic emblem is not to be touched or handled (taboo), is this not somehow impeding its function? Durkheim notes, however, that if it is water, say, that has been made sacred, a person will not drink it unless he has received it from a third party, belonging no doubt to another clan, and who therefore would not be concerned by this particular "taboo." It is possible to overcome the obstacle which bars one from its physical or mystical use. There is no religion without liturgy, but there is no liturgy without sacrament!

And the real process of remembering, like feelings, always imply "mediators": the most elementary of these is making a knot in one's handkerchief, or scattering pebbles along one's path; memories could not last without the external signs which are associated with them (relics, trophies, even monuments or commemorative plates, etc.); thus, in every field, both effective intermediaries and material aids are needed. Besides, language mingles both aspects: the French "souvenir" refers to a "thing" as well as to an event.[16]

Marcel Mauss insists still more strongly than Durkheim on the role and power of exchange in the civilizations he studies: "the thing itself has a soul, he writes, it is a soul. So that by showing something to somebody, one shows a part of oneself.[17]"

As a result, there is nothing more dangerous than a present: the giver thus wields his power on the receiver, who is under his obligation (and who is vassalized). The latter will have to return, somehow or other, as much, or if possible, more than he received—hence the so-called *potlatch* rite.

It is impossible to refuse the "offering," for it would mean refusing

(16) — "un souvenir" means both a memory and a souvenir (Translators' note).
(17) — Marcel Mauss, *Sociologie et anthropologie*, P.U.F., Paris, 1973, pp. 160-161.

communication, alliance. Yet, one is not expected to stop at that (the gift): the idea is to become the obligator of one's obligators. Clan relations, like individual relations, are based on a system of competitive exchange. Social life is entirely structured around restitution and (apparent) offering ceremonies.

Moreover, according to Marcel Mauss, "whole cans [...] of whale-oil are burnt, as well as houses, blankets by the thousand, the most precious pieces of copper are burnt, they are thrown into the sea...[18]" Is this not proof enough that we despise riches and that we happily destroy everything around us upon which we depend for sustenance?

By being extravagant, the spendthrift is in reality demonstrating his power. It is not that he underestimates the value of all these goods, he thus avoids in this manner a siege or a threat by the spirit which might inhabit them, or which might insinuate itself into him via a third party: shortly, if the oil or the clothes are a gift from someone, he will become distrustful and may prefer to burn them. But if they are his personal "belongings" (his house, his tools), he uses fire to prevent his rivals from getting hold of them, and prefers to leave them in the care of the clan's ancestors (by sacrificing them and making them go up in smoke). Whatever the explanation we favour, it confirms the deep-rooted spiritualization of property. Life can only be understood and studied in relation to a flux of objects: for it is on them alone that depends an understanding of the psycho-social spheres.

***

This "object" must be defined, however, before it can be glorified. It must be distinguished from that which it is usually mistaken for, and contrasted with: "the thing." Neither should it be confused with a piece of merchandise, with a part, or with a work.

The object has always been underrated. Sometimes, it is even referred to in terms which are almost insulting—junk, stuff, rubbish, trash, trifles, etc. Slang certainly tends to minimize the things it refers to ("shack" for house, "threads" for clothes, "sack" for bed, etc.). These pejorative terms

(18) — Id., p. 202.

are to be seen in terms of the practise of exorcism or of magic. Similarly, it is well known, Jove starts by praising those he is going to destroy: in order to avoid the anger of the gods, the Ancients depreciated the things to which they were attached, hoping to preserve them this way. That is why one should not take these cunning invectives too seriously!

The fact remains that the word "merchandise," which reduces the thing to what can be "bought" and "sold," completely ignores the very "value" of what is being exchanged, in other words its content. And the same goes for a close synonym: "product"; here, only the manufacturing process is highlighted. Once again, the term does not take into account the raison d'être of the process. Now then, the object is related to a desire; it is moulded on the body and on life. Would a chair have been built and sold if man had not needed to sit and rest? Economic concerns must not blind one totally from anthropological ones.

Such substantives as "part" or "item" are also demeaning since they seem to refer to only one element of the whole, which has been divided up: take the wheel, for instance; only the car ought to be given any consideration. The word "wheel" then, implies that the whole, is a mere fitting together of different parts, and that it has been pulled apart.

I shall return to this conception later, but for the time being, it should not—nor should these terms—lead us to neglect the object itself, in its function of human tool and extension. As a result, it is made to fit man, even if only in size.

This is no longer true of a block of buildings, and still less of the city or the region (which are "meta-objects") in that we cannot grasp them.

A book definitely belongs to the world of objects, but not so definitely—if at all—the bookcase in which it is placed; neither do its characters (neither beyond, nor short of it). Naturally, in both deed and thought, we are able to break anything apart and to put it together again, but by doing so, the delimited "object area" is shaken and becomes confused, since it can be transformed either into a non-seizable super-object, or into an almost invisible micro-object. The same goes for the human body: an arm, or a hand, even the fingers can be isolated in the mind; it can go so far as to isolate each phalanx. At the other extreme, the subject becomes merged in an assembly or a crowd. In the case of merging, the reference, that is the individual body, the only real unit, is abolished. The printed book can be reduced to its pages, its lines, its characters, but it can also be lost in a great mass; however, this type of dislocating mental process does not affect the object's reality principle and its symbiotic relation with man, who recognizes himself in the object: a bookcase is designed especially so that the reader may find the books he wants easily. Thus, the notion of a being (the object) inseparable from its user is gaining strength.

It is true nonetheless that this elementary definition of the object —necessarily including usage, or some form of handling—once again gives it a negative connotation: it places too much emphasis on its utensil-aspect. I shall stress this point later: it should be acknowledged that the object is always understood on a variety of levels; one must not only take into account the prosaic level, but also the possibility to put it up easily, or to fold it up—and one must also not forget those levels which lend an individual, decorative or symbolic meaning to the object...

And yet, Francis Ponge enables us to overrule the former remark, which was somewhat undermining, given precisely the strong utilitarian element in the object: "Littré writes that 'ustensile'[19] comes from *uti (to be of use*, the root of 'outil'[20]) and that it should be spelled and pronounced 'utensile' He adds that there is absolutely no ground for the s, and that it is quite barbaric. But I, on my part, think that it has been added because of the s in '*ostensible*'[21], and that there is nothing barbaric in that; it is, on the contrary, the sign of great understanding. [...] It must be admitted that the word 'ustensile' is in perfect keeping with the character of the object, which hangs on the kitchen wall—for when it is being hung, it swings for a while and oscillates producing rather a shrill sound as it rubs against the wall.[22]" Let us put an end to the trial against usage, for it encourages us to despise unfairly and with too great an ease that which is helpful, when in fact, this kind of censorship should be considered a dangerous consequence of "mentalism."

As for the terms "item," "part," or "element" (false synonyms, but then, are not all synonyms false?), they suggest interchangeability: the

(19) — "Ustensile" is the French for utensil. (Translators' note).
(20) — That is the French for "tool". (Translators' note).
(21) — "Ostensible" means conspicuous. (Translators' note).
(22) — Francis Ponge, "l'Ustensile", in *le Grand Recueil*, Méthodes, Gallimard/N.R.F., Paris, 1961, p. 218.

part is easily mistaken for the whole, whereas the whole is reduced to a sum of divisible parts. We must beware of this tendency if we do not want to deprive the object of its dignity.

It is a good thing, however, that some appliances, or means, can be divided up into their parts. It is sometimes better to replace a part than to attempt to maintain the whole, or give the whole up for lost when it has broken down. One only needs to change the defective part.

The progress of standardization relies on processes of rapid dismantling and reassembly. The tool then becomes a sort of "nest of tables": it is made up of a number of different elements which have been methodically designed to fit into one another, but which can be pulled apart at any time, enabling to fix the broken part. Western thought, however, which owes a great deal to aristotelian thought processes, based on the models of the sculptor, of the carpenter, of the caster, of the potter, would have it that the idea pervades completely the stone, the piece of wood, of metal or of earth. "Form" determines the "substance" through which it is indivisibly spread, and which it elevates. We are at the opposite extreme of the modern system of "parts" which are easily removed and replaced.

Worse still: this kind of work requires a relatively low-qualified workforce, given modern technology's ability to calibrate, number, and lay out the different components of the machine or of the appliance (be it a clock, a gun or a reaper). S. Giedion gives us an explanation for the present "partes extra partes" revolution, which emerged in the United States in the nineteenth century. In this vast country, the user would work far from manufacture and repair centres, so that he himself had to mend and patch up his machine. The result was the emergence of a new association method in construction, based on the use of hinges, pegs and bolts.

"One of the very rare catalogues from the sixties, the *Circular for the Year 1867* of the most elegant constructor of agricultural machinery, Walter A. Wood, Hoosick Falls, N.Y., publishes six "diagrams of parts" for his mower and handrake reaper, each part being illustrated and numbered, so that the farmer need only write for the necessary part by number. From the first, the mechanically minded farmer was accustomed to assemble the machine himself.[23]"

---

(23) — Siegfried Giedion, *Mechanization Takes Command. A Contribution to Anonymous History*, W. W. Norton and Company, New York/London, 1969, p. 50.

Easy, simple, efficient processes are preferred. The object loses its mythical unity, but its durability increases, as well as its possibilities of complex arrangement. It escapes incomprehensibility and displays itself as a structure relying on composition or as a well organized arrangement. The result is the rejection of any whole which is too strongly unified—and too rigid: being, it is commonly admitted, even material being, must partake of inseparability, and that which is born of mere association processes is too easily overlooked.

Conversely, items such as lighters, pens, razors, etc. are disposable: if the user is eager to extend the life of some objects (their very being), he wishes to get rid of others—those mentioned above—as soon as he has used them. That is why there can be no valid unitarian theory encompassing all objects, since it is obvious that all do not belong to the same universe.

Correlatively, in a fairly close field, a number of oppositions arise, due not to the role of objects, but to their location.

Thus, pieces of furniture (which make up another class) are not all the same, but vary according to the place they occupy. The dining-room sideboard is characterized by its respectability, even majesty (in bourgeois or traditionally-minded families), its puritanism (it shelters or hides things away), and the great care which is taken in its upkeep. In the kitchen—a work area—, convenience and domestic organization are the main criteria: it is then said to be "functional" or "modular," since it is made up of bits and pieces. The first cabinet is of patrimonial nature (it is often passed down, adorned with a monogram or with the family seal; it may bear the name or at least the initials of the father); the second cabinet, out of whitewood perhaps, is humbler, and it is to be related to fashion (a concern for style), and to comfort (movement is made easier). So it is absolutely impossible to mistake one for the other.

When our "environment" and our utensils are under attack, when the object is criticized from the point of view of only one of these two dimensions, it is easy to destroy the argument by evoking the second dimension, which is based on opposite principles. This multivalence silences any remarks, negative ones in particular. Positive ones too, one might object. But I do not accept this: how can one not take into account multiplicity? Under theses circumstances, the variety and the richness of our daily environment, inseparable from the culture of an era (time) and of a region (space) must be acknowledged.

But the closest and furthest word from "object" is "thing," that which man has neither conceived nor produced, for instance water, flowers, or stone.

Francis Ponge precisely is guilty of having mixed up the two levels. He extols what is given to man (nature) in the same way as what is brought by man (work, skill). Wasp, fruit, glass of water, bread, candle, cage—all are thrown in together, and generally speaking, he tends to praise the former rather than the latter (*Le Parti pris des choses*).

Those who regard the object with disdain—the object-haters—tend to widen the gap between these two categories; they take advantage of the similarity to confuse the situation, in order to elevate the one and to lower the other. As a result, in practice as in theory, raw materials—such as leather, bark, cotton, wool, wood, earth—are valued by all. On the other hand, competing materials such as glass, steel, cast iron, concrete are condemned, and the same goes for synthetic material—plastics—, most alarming and bitterly criticized of all.

That which is not man-made, but which can only be copied—and not very successfully, besides—or superficially imitated, is thought to be of incomparable depth: who could rival what time has carefully developed (along with the spring sap)? How can man hope to surpass, or even to equal, exuberant, powerful and majestic nature?

Among "material things," wood is the most fervently celebrated: the list of species testifies to this, and is enough to glorify it: oak, ash, beech, walnut, Dutch pine, wild cherry, mahogany, ebony, sycamore, rosewood, etc. Life, it seems, would be impossible without it, because of its warmth, of its softness, of its colour. It is as pleasant to our eye as it is to our hand; it deadens harsh sounds. Besides, its praises have been sung by poets, for instance by Charles Péguy: "Down beneath, the noble resistance, the profound agedness, the mysterious antiquity of nature. Marvellous and deep wood-scent, honest and yet natural, proper and material. The wood's ligneous hardness, just right, varying between the different types of wood, on a scale, according to a well-designed series, according to a harmonious range of degrees, from the softest to the hardest, from whitewood to oak and walnut (boxwood being a precious and low-volume wood..., its

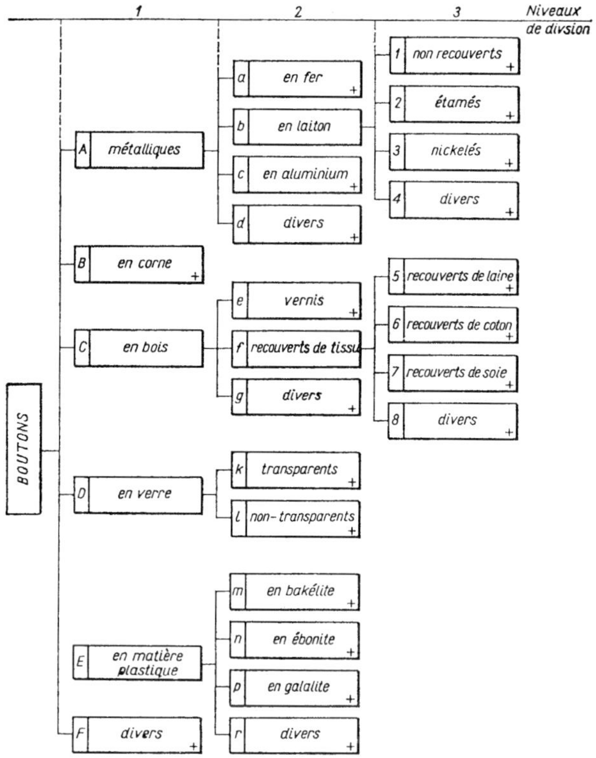

Niveau	1	2	3	Total
Cl. nodales	4	2	0	6
Cl. extrêmes	2	11	8	21
Total	6	13	8	27

8 – This chart allows to substitute numerical or alphanumerical designation for analogical description

diametre width is small, it is knotty and hard, and is used to produce curiosities, not furniture)." And this poem ends on a declaration of war: wood and stone "must unite against modern materials, against metal, reduced to iron, for simplicity's sake. Ancient and close alliance between these two construction materials against modern construction materials."

Both these things come from the heart of the forest (wood), or from the entrails of the earth, from the mine (stone), combine opposites, thus avoiding the uniformity and poorness of formica glass, polystyrene and even of some metals, like zinc, lead or copper; they too have appeared from the dark recesses; but given all the different processes needed to extract them, they evoke industry much more than they do the earth with its veins. Wood and stone can be carved, cut up, chiselled, they demand manipulation, and yet they resist us: let us acknowledge their both hard and docile natures, their sensitivity to that which cuts or chisels.

As for synthetics, they display their own lack of ontological dignity and their ugliness just by attempting to imitate familiar materials; their lack of any real existence or originality allows them, by moulding or by casting themselves, to take any form or role: fake marble, fake grass, fake bronze, fake tortoise-shell, fake fur, etc. It is common knowledge that they are prone to a kind of leprosy: they rapidly grow rigid, yellow, and start to peel.

However, criticism has not prevented them from evolving, nor from being gradually improved: they already have won the battle over their greatest opponents.

The argument between thing and object is not a minor one: at stake is the antinomy between nature and culture, between the world and man who alters it, between submission and victory.

Among other feats, synthetic materials have succeeded in combining extreme qualities; for example lightness, thinness with the highest resistance, or the ability to keep their shape with a suppleness which allows them to be stretched in any direction. At the same time, they have modified the most common gestures or movements (as they do not break when they fall; or require any maintenances such as repainting or waxing). The imagination, even, is stimulated: they may take the shape of liquid paste or light froth on the one hand, of a solid block or of an unchanging rod on the other. They are between categories. The wonders they produce are celebrated by art, which hitherto was exclusively devoted to hard materials, such as stone, bronze or wood. Their remarkable variety ensures that synthetics finally win the battle: natural materials are what they are and never change, whereas "promethean" materials now heighten their inherent qualities, now ally themselves with other materials, producing new qualities (as in the combination, for instance, of the transparency of a given material and the non-inflammable quality of a second one). Let us take this a step further: who would deny the necessity for everything to be processed in order to be usable? Nature can only produce stimulants and means, hence the obligatory and inevitable transition from "thing" to "object." Stone must be hewn and carved, wood must be hollowed and chiselled. Even fruit must be gathered, peeled sometimes, and sliced.

The emphasis should be placed on "doing," thanks to which anything can be made to satisfy our needs, and not on "being." A wide gap between thing and object implies in fact a certain philosophical attitude, based on theological grounds: man is lowered, whilst that which he has not achieved himself is extolled (that which has been given to him by a mysterious force).

The last stratagem intended to discredit the object is to contrast it with the work, the only real product of creation and thus truly original.

Manufactured (or rather machine-made) goods are by definition the result of simple operations, which for the most part consist of assembly: sticking, stamping, screwing, crimping... Another consideration is their chain-production. By contrast, the work—generally made of a piece—requires a skilful executing hand (the craftsman-artist) which bestows upon it its singularity. Literature and culture alike have contributed to widening the gap between the two: the vile object is incomparable with the "handmade product," created thanks to hard work and talent, and related to knowledge and tradition (to a particular school).

This distinction, so widespread that it is held for a truth, is highly questionable.

First, it should be reminded that, even in the workshop of the classical painter, tasks were divided and mechanized. Several painters worked together to produce the final picture: the painter who specialized in bouquets worked alongside the one who specialized in portraits or in animals (dogs or horses). And in some cases, the master of the "workshop" would do no more than sketch out the painting, which he would then sign. He would touch it up and add the finishing touches— but his main function was as the painting's guarantee.

And even those artists who work alone are subjected to a certain amount of repetition: almost all have had to tirelessly start over again that which they had begun; or they have become obsessed by a particular "theme," "perspective," or "motif" (a flower, a haystack, a cathedral, a landscape). In short, working in "series" or endlessly resuming the same thing was not abhorrent to them.

And what is more, at the bottom of the manufacturing and the creative process alike undoubtedly lies some kind of "conjuring act," "illusion" or "trick." But it has been to the great advantage of artists to render their work mysterious and to leave their secrets in the dark, so that they have spread this false legend.

"[...] I would rather compose a mediocre work and remain lucid than a brilliant masterpiece in a trance-like state [...] For a brilliant flash will get me nowhere [...] I find the ability to produce even the tiniest spark which has been dictated to me by my will, infinitely more interesting than the need to wait in order to project the flashes of lightning, which might or might not occur every now and then.[24]" These are the words of a dissident: of a man who has rejected the traditional myth of the artist.

Finally, the object is viewed as a work which has been produced hastily, hence its multiple samples, whereas the work is viewed as a rare object. It may be true that one of them is easier to find than the other— however one ought not to turn "quantity" into the sign of an ontological difference!

Besides, industry, by which art is later inspired, does not only provide us with immutable and gloomy productions: on the contrary, its aim is to alter and renew them. And if a distinction had, at all costs, to be made, it is the craftsman-artist's work which is prone to repetition (for hardly any innovation is involved) whereas the factory-chain, manufacturing processes perpetually undergo alteration and rationalization.

(24) — Paul Valéry, "Fragments et mémoires d'un poème", in *Variété*, book 5, N.R.F., Paris, 1945, p. 102.

Moreover, when it does not alter the product, industry changes its external marks, thanks to which it may be remarked. And in my opinion, packaging, labels, and all the signs which give the product its individuality are to be considered important.

Advertising art has made goods more and more attractive and original. At times, today's object is drowned by the images which are attached to it: one need not look very far (an extreme example is a piece of clothing covered with advertisement logos) to see that each object is the bearer of distinctive signs, of greater appeal to the buyer than the object's usefulness. These signs are either sown, stuck or incorporated in one way or another (in silkscreen printing, the sign is "welded" to the object: Andy Warhol's beloved Coca-Cola label is printed on—and hence one with—the glass bottle itself).

Besides, one of the constant features of present production is that the container assumes greater significance than the contents (in the acquisition of a pair of shoes, a tie, a shirt, the label is of greater importance than the object which it adorns and of which it is the guarantee —in this way, the buyer displays his power and his "class").

When the object cannot undergo a metamorphosis, the packaging is changed. Somebody reticent or opposed to this argument would declare this to be dupery since all one is doing is trading on appearance—and he would add that the more one alters the "decoration," the less one alters the product which is being commercialized.

I cannot subscribe to this kind of criticism, nor can I accept the partitions which some have attempted to establish, the aim being to smash the object to pieces and to devalue it. Where, indeed, does the outer layer of the object begin? Take the "pen" for example: it is essentially made up of that which encompasses the nib as well as the cartridge (the refill). The body of this container is inseparable from that which it encloses and unites, and cannot be distinguished from the contents—thus making apparent the importance of what is regarded as a mere capsule. That which solidarizes, includes and protects is part of the instrument, just as are the more active and operational parts. In short, let us renounce all divisions and wholeheartedly bind the inside to the outside.

***

Even once the object has been distinguished from its neighbours—goods, things, parts and works of art and craft—, it still escapes a straightforward understanding, given its many different levels (ranging from the utilitarian to the symbolic).

In order to grasp it—at least in its outline—more clearly, it is necessary to have recourse to classification, although it is true that this method tends to be discredited because it is reminiscent of the museum curator, whose job is to arrange and store, as well as of a mania for order and compilation. However, this method will help us define the singularity of this specimen or that, and at the same time will throw some light on the expanse of the world of objects. An understanding may be reached only in the consideration of the whole, by taking into account any differences and their typology. Each unit has its own particular constituent parameters. It is essential therefore to grasp the "phylum" in order to determine the position on the board of such or such creation: and taking this chess-metaphor still further, "style" corresponds to a position on the grid of the relations between the elements.

Different methods may be used to catalogue things. Currencies, for instance, may be classified according to chronological order (date of issue), to the mint (the place rather than the period), or else to the stamp (iconography); in these cases however, (arbitrary) filing is being mistaken for classification (aiming at the definition of the inherent principle of classification). The latter alone is of any use for it enables us to reconstruct the whole group.

Let us make a grid. Since domestic objects are at the centre of the present discussion, let us start by taking a look at the distribution of different pieces of furniture: what taxonomic method will enable us to sort the different chests, tables, dressers, cabinets, beds, cupboards, clocks, kneading-troughs, benches, chests of drawers, writing desks, chairs, armchairs, and so on? How does one plan, and where does one divide? How does one deal with such a vast number of objects? According to which principles does one locate these pieces of furniture, in order to appreciate them better?

Suzanne Tardieu suggests an appropriate way to divide them: she distinguishes two large groups: those pieces of furniture which are designed to support (the exterior prevails over the interior), and those which contain (the inside prevails). Space as a criterion for division is a sufficiently generic explanation. According to Suzanne Tardieu, virtually nothing falls in both groups at the same time, so that nothing is liable to impede this partition or to make it ineffective: "A few pieces of furniture belong to both sets; they are small in number and one of their two functions always prevails, so that it is possible to connect them to one of the branches of study.[25] "

Let us restrict ourselves now to those pieces of furniture which contain other objects (linen, food, dishes, records, etc.) and which it would be appropriate to call "meta-objects."

The contents may often be enough to constitute or characterize the container—this I would gladly concede, since it confirms the complementarity of inside and outside: the salt-chair contains the salt, the bread basket the bread, the larder the food, and cupboards, wardrobes and chests of drawers are filled with linen or documents. Down a level, turning from furniture to utensils, the same duality becomes apparent: here too, we are in the presence of cavities which are one with their contents.

The container's main function—to isolate and to shelter—is never called into question, no matter whether it serves an extremely specific purpose, or whether on the contrary, its purpose is completely unspecified (so that it contains the most varied substances indiscriminately). Be that as it may, "function" should not be considered a criterion of classification. I wish only to point out the great variety of "boxes," and the astounding number of forms they take. And above all, the first, quasi-geometric, criterion at the base of our classification system, must be kept: is it a plane, or a cavity (a closed shape)? In the first case, the main constituent element is either a horizontal surface (a table top), or a hard base (the bed), or a vertical plane (the dresser) which both displays objects in an upright position and supports them. As for the second subset, that which contains, a supplementary device is necessary: either a lid, or a door, or a drawer.

Some dressers might be said to confuse this first partition, but in fact they merely combine the two possibilities: the lower and main part—

(25) — Suzanne Tardieu, *le Mobilier rural traditionnel français*, Aubier-Flammarion, Paris, 1976, p. 45.

which may have two or three doors—contains objects for daily use, whereas the top displays objects of value—dishes, plates, and jugs. Thus, both functions—protection and display—appear side by side.

The sideboard generally combines the two as well: although it complicates the grid, it does not challenge it. If it is low to the ground, it includes a working surface (which, when raised, ensures that the sideboard becomes almost identical to the chest) on which is placed that which is being served, whereas inside are put away objects which are fragile or which one can do without. In this case then, the sideboard contains at the same time as it supports, thus merging both functions.

There may be a third "combination": the sideboard may consist of two "bodies" which might sometimes be of a piece (separated nonetheless in the middle by a set of drawers, placed at the level for a man). And if there is a recess between the two, which might as well be the case, a new combination appears (though not a hybridization). Between the upper and the lower containers, there may be an open space, so that what is placed there is no longer hidden. Side by side once again are an "inside" which prevails and an "outside" which although reduced is still present (see figure 1 for an illustration of this duality). It is obvious that the volume of this open space, in which that which is to remain visible is placed, is greater when the two bodies (the lower and the upper ones) are more independent of each other; this is the case when only the legs of the upper body are in contact with the lower body (see fig. 2)[26]. Besides, the whole scale of possibilities is covered between absolute compactness and sheer separation. Finally, although the two groups that we have contrasted (the inside and the outside) never merge completely, they continually meet and intersect.

Hence, it may be concluded that every piece of furniture is made to exploit to the full the spatial possibilities, to which it is adapted and which it highlights. It conforms to, occupies and renders complex its axes. On the one hand, it reckons on division for its existence and its singularity, but on the other hand, it joins and makes whole again that which has been split for functional purposes (as in displaying and hiding).

It has been established in passing that the dresser and the sideboard

(26) — The main parts may of course be virtually inseparable; one of them is then stuck in the other one, as is shown in fig. 3

both combine two functions; but it is possible for these two mixtures to be combined yet again, as is shown by figure 4 (a dresser and a sideboard are "joined" together, so to speak, although the latter tends to "invade" the display shelf so that it is filled with drawers as well as small cupboards on each side).

Although the first spatial criterion defined (namely enclosure and the preference given to the inside) may sometimes be connected with its opposite (the supporting surface), it nevertheless allows us to discriminate between two main branches.

However, once separated, those pieces of furniture of which it is the function to protect take on an astounding variety: therefore, it is necessary to proceed further in the analysis of distribution; but how?

When they are made up of two main bodies, these may well be of disproportionate sizes: the upper body may be reduced in size, whereas the lower one may be voluminous (see fig. 5), or, conversely, the lower part may be small in comparison with the upper part, a rarer variant, which occurs nonetheless (see fig. 6). In the first and more frequent case, the minimization of the upper part may be extreme and may even forbid the use of a "door" or of a traditional shutting device, which is replaced by a "sliding panel" (for enclosure).

Another kind of disparity might not be between the upper and the lower parts this time, but between both sides, giving rise to a dissymmetry. In this case, only one enclosure remains, on one side, unless it is placed in the centre in order to restore symmetry (in some areas, the centre is often designed to fit a clock). (see fig. 7).

According to the choice of the particular axis, either vertical or horizontal, certain parts become more prominent than others, thus giving rise to noticeable differences between models. And we have only considered the case of the "two-bodied" sideboard: for each of its two containers, it would be useful to list its morpho-genetic and structural elements. In addition to this qualitative classification should come numerical assessment (height, width, depth, intervals, etc.)

It must be pointed out that enough attention has not been given to that which singularizes the object and which allows one to situate it: embellishments, mouldings, ornamental ironwork, hinges, maybe even marquetry, the very nature of the wood, and trimmings...

There are three good reasons for drawing up such a vast grid:

a) The first is that any part or any sample can be placed within the grid, and thus, precisely defined. It is even possible to issue hypotheses regarding "filiation" or "influence" between the constituent units.

b) It is also possible to locate "blanks" (or virtual blanks) which a creator might decide to fill (he might do innovating work in these areas), although contemporary designers are generally less interested in completing a group than in altering its traditional lines and revolutionizing its structure.

c) This grid also allows us to recognize the various properties of the object (pieces of furniture, for the time being): those of arrangement, fairly close to those of style, which cannot be identified with those utilitarian ones, to which too much attention is paid. Cabinet-makers and joiners have made very different use of volume and assembling techniques. This is made obvious in their different cutting and cleaving methods.

Synoptic charts are of great help for the production theorist: they will enable him, in passing, to substitute elliptical designations for more commonly used terms, which are often vague and loose.

Any object can be divided into its specific components, as Zygmunt Dobrowolski has shown in his book on classification systems.[27] He gives numerous examples of new types of codification and suggests the dividing up of goods, means of transport, and even "buttons" into vast and heterogeneous groups.

In the case of buttons, Dobrowolski first considers the substance they are made of: A for metal; B for horn; C for wood; D for glass; E for plastic; F for "miscellaneous substances." This kind of logical tree is followed by a more accurate analysis of the kind of wood, or metal. With regard to metal, a) stands for iron; b) for brass; c) for aluminium; d) for any other metal. Lastly, in the third subgroup comes the coating (tin- or nickel-plated, etc.), so that in the end, he comes up with Ab2, for example, which refers to a metal button made of tin-plated brass (see fig. 8).

Three characters have replaced at least five words. As a result of this rapid mnemonic process, description is minimized and pride of place is

(27) — Zygmunt Dobrowolski, *Etude sur la construction des systèmes de classification,* Gauthier-Villars, Paris, 1964.

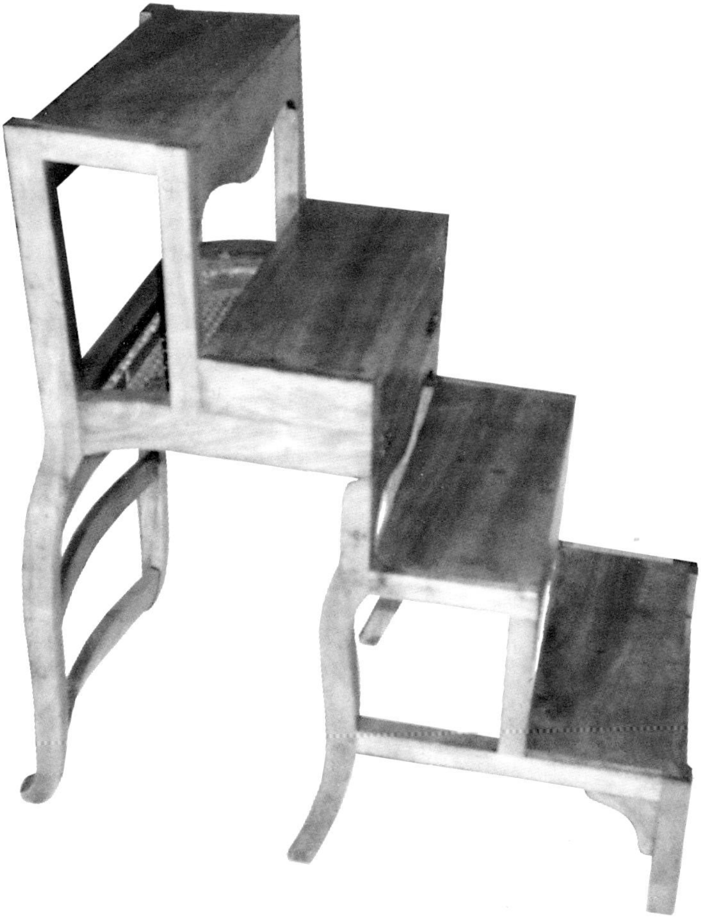

9 – A transformable piece of furniture designed during the French Restoration

given to organized and hierarchic presentation. The whole group can be thrown onto a mere sheet of paper: any unit can be easily included. The order (that is, the classes and their branches) is immediately apparent.

***

The object has been carefully defined and its anatomy described. However, an inquiry into its situation is not enough. We must proceed further. There are so many strata, so many levels in it!

Apart from the utilitarian level, which receives the most attention, the technical one, divided into two branches should not be neglected (which mechanical devices were used, and how was the object made?), nor should the following: the formal or morphological levels, which cannot be separated from the taxonomic one (the present cleavage between form and function will be further discussed, and the age-long belief, fostered by the Bauhaus, in particular, that one of these elements necessarily determines the other one will be dismissed); the decorative, the historical levels (the function of an object may change in the course of its development; the object may even gradually disappear), the symbolic, the poetical, the ergonomic levels (how has man made an object safer and easier to use?), the strictly physical level (what material should be used?), the lexicographical level (the various names and nicknames that might be used to refer to the object), the identifying level (giving information: where and when it was produced, for instance, or the "best before" date for perishable goods, etc.), the emblematic level (the designer's label, or the owner's name-tag, which is like a coat of arms).

So it is difficult to understand why the object has been discredited and forgotten for so long. It seems though, that today, this prejudice is being called into question; man has renounced narcissism: the object has made an entrance in art and is now granted a major status; and art, in turn, has begun to govern the object and to play a role in its manufacture (ugliness, it is well-known, is difficult to sell).

The thousand-year old division between the fine arts and the mechanical arts, between the cult of beauty and that of usefulness, between the noble and the prosaic is coming to an end.

CHAPTER II

The logic of representative art

It may seem presomptuous to venture into an outline of the history of art, and still more so to endeavour to discover a clear-cut trend in today's art, which is said to be so multifaceted. Let us hope that this excessiveness will be forgiven on both counts.

Worse still, what follows are purely elementary remarks; in order for one not to find them shockingly simplistic, it is necessary to rid oneself first of all the notions one has been fed in this field: with a great deal of amphigory, of references to the so-called "meanings" that art supposedly conveys through its complex achievements, the correlative emergence of gurus whose claim is to understand that which will always escape the layman. Without wishing to deny its great stature, the work of art does not deserve this kind of pseudo-dramatization. Each "creation" requires a close and patient scrutiny, and cannot be grasped by rapid or casual surveys. This approach will not be adopted here, however. Instead, it seems more appropriate to outline a vast sketch, taking us from yesterday's art to that of today, and including a description of what is to come.

Whatever the current opinion, art is wholly informed by a kind of dialectics: there are no spontaneous, or unexpected changes of style; each new style is opposed to the former one, and tolls its death. There is nothing more murderous, or more transient.

This is a point Hegel clearly grasped when he emphasized the necessary succession of "ages" or moments. "Progress" is the wrong word since today's art is no improvement on yesterday's, nor does it push the latter to the background; "cumulative revolutions," implying that they follow and influence each other, seems more appropriate. Only an immanent and rational logic may account for this evolving history.

Hegel's basic thesis is that the beautiful refers to the incarnation of the spirit in matter: the art object thus externalizes thought; it merges the supra-sensible with the sensible, and, by doing so, it operates a transfiguration.

It is perfectly clear that in the beginning, with symbolic art, the organizing principle is somewhat overwhelmed by materiality (hence, among other things, the massive, complex, ornate, oriental temple). Classicism however achieves a new balance: the Greeks are a case in point, as their architecture shows (simple and harmonious), as does their sculpture (which depicts gods, like Apollo, so different from the superhuman and violent Titans). The symbiosis between soul and matter has never been so successful. One is still fascinated by such harmony and such serene proportions. However, the spirit's inevitable aim is freedom and sovereignty, it is to overcome matter—and this is the third stage of Hegel's description; the result is romantic art, and a tendency for materiality to become lighter and less intrusive.

The necessity of these three stages is easy to understand: for after the age of overwhelming and massive achievements, followed by that of equilibrium, comes the apotheosis and the victory of the emerging spirit (in Dutch painting in particular, which is so suggestive, due to the choice of the smallest possible canvas and to the concentration on the interplay between light and shade).

An understanding of art cannot be reached through monographs or through individual analysis: it must be considered as a whole, and every stage of the creation to its fulfilment must be grasped in its movement.

Thus, it will become apparent that the underlying aspiration of art is to get to grips with reality—not to dominate it, but simply to celebrate it. The artist takes on the role of "officiating priest": he performs the ceremony whereby that which has been forgotten, or even disregarded, is restored; he warns us of any threat (evil, the downfall or alienation of society, corruption), he heralds the promises of a world to come, and he shows us how to rid ourselves of blinkers and of our narrow-mindedness. Art is thus comparable to a religious service based on a revelation, and to a common practice which brings salvation and redemption.

***

The painter (for it is he, who is at the centre of the discussion) once played a more humble role than he does today: in the beginning, long before he started to make use of wood and canvas, he would transpose fleeting reality onto a cave wall. By doing so, he hoped to capture, to commemorate and to embellish it. The aim was to overcome absence, or to avert danger.

The Ancients tell us that a young girl, who was in great distress because her beloved had to leave her and go to war, chalked out his silhouette on a wall. In doing so, she was attempting to immobilize the outlines of his body in order to preserve its shape. Hunters would also sketch out on stones their trophies, or simply the beasts they hoped to catch; in this manner, they would record their most memorable catches and their victorious fights, as well as, at the same time, ensure success in a future hunt.

After these rather prosaic beginnings, "scenography" was to know no bounds, one of its chief purposes being to remind us of the main religious scenes (the Annunciation, the Last Supper, The Presentation in the Temple...), and later on, of royal scenes (a coronation) or of military ones (a naval fight, the capture of a stronghold). Then emerges the "portrait," either that of a ruler (a dynasty), or an emblematic representation of a whole guild.

Pictorial representation fulfils a vital function, namely as a memory tool and a celebration of the most important moments, which are repeated and thus transfigured (through a particular focus). Such is the definition of the glorious first period of art (there are four in all, tightly knit by a shared logic).

In spite of such clear goals and such a straightforward guiding principle, art, in this period, is afflicted by a number of problems pertaining to its technical execution. Let us mention some of these:

a) The first is related to the effectiveness of the reconstituting process: the trees in these pictures resemble bushes of quivering branches and leaves. A figure's hair is rendered in such a way, as though the artist has drawn each one, one by one.

How, with a few rapid brush-strokes, can the painter successfully give the illusion that he has faithfully reproduced the infinite, the innumerable, without leaving anything out? The moiré of velvet, the grain of the skin, the tiny pebbles on the road, the grass clumps in the meadow, the slight undulation of water can be made visible. How is it possible to reduce without diminishing? How is it possible to depict the endlessness of the world without drastically reducing it or depriving it of its nuances, with so little and within such a tiny space (the canvas)?

This question is very complex since too much precision may prevent the effect after which the artist strives. Ernst Gombrich has a clear grasp of the problem with its stumbling blocks, and makes a suggestion to help us solve the difficulty: "We have the impression that he painted every stitch of the golden damask, every hair of the angel, every fibre of the wood. Yet he clearly could not have done that, however patiently he worked with a magnifying glass. Little though we may know about the secrets of such effects, they must be based on an illusion.

I believe that this illusion is assisted by what might be called the "etc. principle," the assumption we tend to make that to see a few numbers of a series is to see them all.[1]"

This explains why too many details may impair the result. A complete rendering must be suggested, but not achieved. The artistic illusion is created by blurred and hazy images. It is precisely through this "fuzziness" that the beginnings of a series needing completion can be perceived (an inceptive alignment or reiteration).

This point is worth stressing because the problem of "representation" is related to the history of technical skills and processes. Let us do away with any theoretical deviances or obscurities: it is the "deed" only that counts.

b) The painter is confronted with an even greater difficulty; as long as this one has not been solved, the aesthetics of appropriation—intended to be a memory aid—cannot evolve. The aim is still to avoid simplification of the universe; the painter must suggest the third dimension within and in spite of a two-dimensional space (the plane canvas surface) for he cannot leave out depth.

Artists have long used empirical methods such as tiles of different size: the illusion of proximity of the foreground is created by the larger tiles, which appear to advance towards one, by contrast to the smaller tiles. Similarly, since distant things look smaller, the way to convey to the spectator the impression of distance is to represent in reduced format some of the elements which in fact have the same size (figures as well as houses and trees).

---

(1) — Ernst H. Gombrich, *Art and Illusion*, Phaidon Press, Oxford, 1960, p.184

Another basic technique is to hide one house behind another, thus demonstrating that one precedes the other, and establishing the idea of graduation. Placing a mirror inside a house is also a most frequent and effective device: the hidden part of the foreground is thus revealed, whilst at the same time a certain distance and detachment is achieved, since one is able to perceive both sides of that which is being represented. In this way, the painter is able to overcome sheer "two-dimensionality."

Artists have always managed to find tricks which give the impression of relief or of distance. The Renaissance was to discover the true method, which supplanted all the old recipes: Brunelleschi discovered the laws of "linear perpective," the principle of this technique being that parallel lines convey the illusion of convergence as they grow more and more distant and finally meet at the horizon: hence the ability to set the latter at a particular distance, or even to move it forward if need be. Alberti also invented "aerial perspective," a technique in which shapes and colours become blurred as they grow distant.

Three-dimensional transcription was even made easier by Dürer, who used the light-room: a given scene, observed through an apparatus containing a minute hole, is projected onto a surface; this apparatus enables one to make an exact copy, to trace outlines, and even to calculate the size of an object in relation to another, given their respective positions in space (the difference between this apparatus and the so-called "camera obscura" being that the former works in the daylight). The problem is thus solved: instead of conforming to the object itself for its depiction, one conforms to the principles of optics, which have been mastered and which may be exploited. In this way, the principles of "representative illusion" establish themselves: "seeing" alters "being" (that which is).

c) Yet, artists were to be hindered by another obstacle, which was nearly insurmountable, stemming from the content itself.

How can one depict or render moral qualities or supernatural phenomena? Since the image-creators generally work for the Church, how will they be able to portray God, the Holy Spirit, the Angels, in a word, the invisible? Is it possible to suggest that which transcends us without succumbing to paganism (to the golden calf or to fetichism)? Patrons encourage an art of "manifestation," whilst at the same time condemning anything that might degrade the sacred or give human shape to it (idolatry).

The representation of Christ also gives rise to a difficult problem: to depict him as a beautiful adolescent—an Adonis —, is just as offensive as it is to show him in a poor or destitute state.

The Greek canons have always held enormous sway over artists: as in the depiction of Christ, almost identical with Apollo, or with Orpheus, who plays the flute and enchants the wild animals from his rock (hence, probably, the "Holy Shepherd," the shepherd with his lamb, evocative of Hermes Criophoros, the one who carries a ram). The scene of the Last Supper is also clearly evocative of the traditional banquet or feast; Moses, as he removes his sandals before climbing the mountain on which God is to speak to him, repeats the gesture of Empedocles as he prepares to climb Mount Etna. The reappropriation of these scenes contributes to the "subduing" and the "paganizing" of the Christian drama.

Is it possible to avoid heresy under these circumstances? Indeed, it is essential not to betray the duality of the lineage: the artist either accentuates the divine aspect (monophysism absorbs or does away with humanity), or else he commits the opposite error and places too little emphasis on divine nature. In both cases, it is a failure.

The painter often finds, it is true, a way of evading the problem: he places Jesus Christ in the distance, amidst a crowd. Or else, he depicts him as a child, with yet unformed traits (the Nativity); or else, the scene of the Ascension allows him to place the Christ in a sort of floating white haze. Concrete representation is avoided in this manner. The believer however cannot be fully satisfied by the mere rendering of an "atmosphere" (as if allusion had taken the place of illusion).

And what of the Crucifixion, which cannot be ignored, nor minimized? The display of gaping wounds and bleeding flesh, as well as that of nudity, is held to be the sign of disrespect. So that in fact, the artist prefers to deal with the legendary past, and remains faithful to the splendid Hellenic art and spirit (the many triumphant and luminous Apollos), or to the depiction of Christ as King, in all his majestic glory (already pantocrator). In spite of himself, he cannot bring himself to represent a dead divinity. As a result of this superimposition and this renewal of the ancient tradition, the artist has gone astray and the supernatural effect is lost.

I do not wish to place too much stress on Christian art as such: it gives one the opportunity, merely, to highlight the "dramas of representation." At any rate, to express the infinite by means of the finite seems impossible: for inevitably, one falls into the disappointing trap of "reification."

One's doubts as to the above mentioned possibility, it must be admitted, are aggravated further in the representation of Angels, of the Holy Spirit, or even of God himself. It is essential that these appear in the painting, yet sickly sentimentality (or conventional scenes) on the one hand, and prosaism or esoteric symbolism on the other, must at all costs be avoided.

It is of no particular interest to list all the different ways around the problem. It is only worth noting, perhaps, that the Roman Catholic Church gets itself out of this predicament by demanding that the artist give a literal rendering of the Scriptures: this is the only acceptable way to represent the Divinity. The Church requires—or rather tolerates—that the Holy Spirit be represented by a dove or else by the tongues of fire above the heads of the Apostles. Any other version is banned; and so too, with even greater severity, is any kind of unorthodox embellishment: "In the Holy Gospel written by the Saints Matthew, Luke and Marc, in the passage that relates the Baptism... (it is mentioned) that the Holy Spirit descended onto our Lord in bodily shape, as a dove." Orthodox art takes hold of the account and immobilizes it. The iconography might undergo refinement, but it cannot deviate from it.

The seventeenth century is less prone to exercises in religious translation than it is to psychological analysis; and yet it comes up against a comparable problem, given that the question remains the same: how to depict a particular passion on the face or in the attitude of a given figure? At the Ecole des Beaux-Arts, of which he was director, Charles Le Brun taught his pupils the correspondence between the body and the emotions, in view of gaining greater pictorial expressiveness and thus avoiding errors, such as a spy with an overly naive face, or an innocent figure with criminal traits.

For a long time, and up until the threshold of the nineteenth century, art continued to fulfil the function of "faithful appropriation" of reality. It is passionately attached to reality which it transposes whilst simultaneously throwing light on it—or rather embellishing it—and which it serves to recall. After the eclipse of religious drama or scenography follow events to be remembered, portraits, or the depiction of favourite spots—in other words, the tide of naturalism.

***

With the nineteenth century, everything changes, and with it, we enter into the second stage of the analysis. For the importance of the technical and material upheavals cannot be overemphasized, in my opinion. The theory of the artist-manufacturer has already been elaborated. So it comes as no surprise that the expansion of methods of reproduction puts an end to the "art of memory." The machine replaces man—at a lower cost—in his most noble and sacred activity: the ability to commemorate and to commit to memory. Not long ago, the copyist who calligraphed the Holy Scriptures was moved to the sidelines by the printing press: similarly, the painter is ruthlessly supplanted by the photograpic industry (the daguerreotype), which was to incense Baudelaire, who believed it to be a symptom of decline.

The artist, ousted by photography, soon uncovers an inhexaustible universe which machines cannot—yet—reach. He gives up portrait-painting and the depiction of important moments of our lives, which he easily renounces since in return he finds new and better subjects. These more than compensate for his loss. In addition, photography hurriedly takes on the role that it had wrested from the artist: in order to ensure that he had well and truly been "evicted," it too begins to produce "pictures," thus imitating the results of the art which it has replaced.

The revolution that follows allows one to better perceive why contemporary plastic art—or "object-art"—cannot be separated from the context of its whole history and its upheavals.

As has already been alluded, this second period is characterized by the exploration of new areas and by the use of new techniques. When the artist has exhausted a given exploratory field, or possibility, he is forced back into exile and must search for new corners, if not for new continents into which to delve. Art lives by and for the sake of renewal (originality is the new law before which it bends); recycling that which has already been used is a recipe for failure.

The opening victory of the second, extremely fruitful period goes to the Impressionist movement: it rushes into that which the daguerreotype cannot possibly capture. And what a victory! It gives one access to a phosphorescent world of optical enchantment; it leaves aside stasis (shape and outlines) and positivism, in favour of imprecision, vapours and mists, and of colour, which escaped photography at the time.

The origin of the movement's name is common knowledge: in *Le Charivari* of 1874, the critic Louis Leroy published an indictment of the paintings exhibited in the salon on Boulevard des Capucines, in which the outcast or rejected artists were grouped. His article was entitled: "The Impressionist Exhibition," a phrase coined after Claude Monet's painting *Impression soleil levant*[2], 1872. It was meant as a pejorative term, implying that the artist had withdrawn into himself, a subjective retinal vision, whereas according to the critic, the artist should open himself to the world.

"A trying day it was, on which I ventured into the first Exhibition on Boulevard des Capucines." And he thundered forth against the exhibition which had been an attack on the high standards of art, on the obligatory respect of form, and on the veneration of the great masters. The school was also referred to as the "School of patches," "the School of eyes," or "the School of the open air," or even "painting for communards."

We are faced with resolute anti-academism: whilst the daguerreotype (the rival instrument) could not yet render colour, painting revealed itself as capable of suggesting the slightest nuance, fleetingness, as well as the most subtle interplay of light.

For these artists of light, landscapes were the dominant motif, which is why they worked in the open air, with great briskness (in order to capture the aerial, ephemeral, evanescent qualities of the atmosphere). Furthermore the colour schemes they chose were vibrant and surpassed nature itself (thanks to the technique of juxtaposed strokes of which Chevreul has shown the importance).

The School of Barbizon (a small town in the Fontainebleau forest) preceded them in the choice of landscape. As the wood was being threatened by the cutting of trees in the name of early industrial demands (for furnaces, mines, the first railway lines), in sign of protestation, these

(2) — *Impression of the rising sun* (Translators' note).

artists started to paint "lone trees," which were no longer "still-lifes," but the exhibition of a solitary, majestic oak, paintings devoid of (human) content.

Until then, the object has played a restricted role in iconography. It now enters into art through the back door of a revolt.

Using different methods and fighting a different battle, Cubism offers a novel—if not an impossible—vision: multiperspectivism or simultaneous vision, which no reproduction process could ever achieve.

Why not attempt to show the box of matches or the musical instrument under all its angles at the same time, from above and below, from the front and from behind, in profile and from the side?

Guillaume Apollinaire wrote: "Cubism is the name given to the new School of painting; it was given in derision by Henri Matisse in the autumn of 1908, just after having seen a painting representing houses of which the cubic appearance struck him deeply. [...] In representing reality-as-conceived, or reality-as-created, the painter can create the illusion of three-dimensionality, he can "*cubify*" so to speak. He would not be able to do so were he simply rendering reality-as-seen.[3]"

Apollinaire was even able to distinguish between different tendencies in this nebulous field: scientific Cubism, physical Cubism, orphic Cubism and instinctive Cubism, all of which share the same aim—namely the reconstruction of the whole, using simple element-units. Since the idea is to overcome retinal vision, fragmentation, allied with multiplication, is the order of the day: it dictates the choice of the different perspectives and their disposal in relation to each other. Imitation is no longer the aim of painting, it aims instead at becoming "a thing in itself," and is no longer satisfied with pure appearance.

This must be stressed because throughout the various transformations undergone by art, an indisputable logic manifests itself. Progress is not an issue since we all know of mediocre painters who go along with modern movements on the one hand, and talented traditionalists on the other, who reject modernity. But exceptions should not be taken as a rule: most real creators combine genius with the dialectical relation to art just described.

(3) — Apollinaire, in *les Peintres cubiques, Oeuvres complètes*, edited by Michel Décaudin, André Balland and Jacques Lecat, Paris, 1966, p. 23.

Cubism, then, discovered a working area in which the machine could not compete (even if and when it could bring together the given elements); it fought a battle against the art of the first period (illusionist painting) and made the first steps towards the recognition of the object (sketching volume on a flat surface).

A new upheaval now takes place: the artist's efforts now direct themselves towards shaking painting out of its stasis. From the moment that Cubism introduces the possibility of three-dimensionality, many painters dream of bringing time or movement into their work (proto-kinetic art)!

Once again, it is science that gives the push, since at the time, Etienne Marey's instrumental research is applied to the "moving image." The Futurists soon start to exploit this breakthrough. The term "Futurism" does not express any reservations, nor is it intended as derogatory. It is taken from Marinetti's article published in *Le Figaro* on the 20th February, 1909: "We launch from Italy into the world this our manifesto of overwhelming and incendiary violence, with which today we found *Futurism*, because we want to liberate this land from the fetid cancer of professors, archaeologists, guides and antiquarians...[4]"

It was not the first time that artists had wanted to render energy, movement and speed: think of Géricault's depiction of horses in full gallop. Now, however, dynamism must become more intense: cinematographic techniques, like those of photography in the past, means that the visual arts are vulnerable once more.

As is always the case with each new upheaval—for history repeats itself—, there immediately begins a series of battles taking issue over this new art form.

"Look at Nicolas Poussin's *Enlèvement des Sabines*[5]": nowhere else is it possible to find such tumultuousness. It is not the image of tumultuousness, but tumultuousness itself... They (modern artists) think that they are resuscitating sculpture, which until their advent was as if injected with curare, irrefragably trapped inside a stone or bronze coating, and that they are restoring it to mobile life. There is, however, a basic idea that

(4) — Quoted in *Concepts of Modern Art*, edited by Nikos Stangos, Thames and Hudson, London, reprinted 1990, p. 98 (Translators' note).
(5) — *The Rape of the Sabines* (Translators' note).

totally escapes them. Statues and painting are static creations. Indeed; but when they are the product of an inspired hand, it is this very stasis which leads to an intense feeling of mobility. This is the capital secret, the great mystery. A statue which is mechanically set in motion is a mere automaton. A painting where the elements move is merely a cartoon.[6]"

Neo-kinetic art continues nonetheless: it concentrates on movements which are imperceptible to the naked eye (Calder), or virtual ones (Vasarely)—so called because they cannot occur without the active participation of the spectator who reconstructs the work.

No one grasped Calder's originality more acutely than Jean-Paul Sartre: "Movement is not merely suggested, it is caught; he does not consider for a moment casting it definitively in bronze or in gold, those celebrated and stupid materials, destined by nature to remain immobile. Instead, with such flimsy and low materials as small bones, tin-plate or zinc, he builds strange constructions: shafts with palms, discs, feathers and petals. In fact, they are resonators and traps, which hang from a string, like a spider from its thread...[7]"

Now most certainly would be a good time to evoke abstract art (with its main trends: geometric abstraction, lyrical abstraction), which is the expression of the painter's attempt to go beyond figurative representation in order to reach the very essence of phenomena.

Nevertheless, I will remain with the three movements of liberation which allow artists to free the canvas from its initial limits—impressionism, Cubism, kinetic art, or, in other words, the successful capture of volatility, multi-perspectivism and movement.

It goes without saying that abstract art shares the same vocation, which it fulfils with still greater energy: it explores all given phenomena —but in order to discover a fundamental world-structure (noumenology), without yielding to optical distortions.

This is not an analysis, it is a caricature, an oversimplification. There are many remarkably learned and subtle minds who dig deep into the work they may be researching, patiently uncovering its foundations, perceiving its every minor detail, who would condemn, and rightly so, the casualness of this approach.

---

(6) — Robert Rey, *Contre l'art abstrait*, 1957.

(7) — Jean-Paul Sartre, "les Mobiles de Calder," in *Situations III*, Gallimard/NRF, Paris, 1949, p. 307.

But are they not losing sight of the whole by concentrating on every detail of creation and by choosing the path of exhaustive analysis? Are they able to connect everything together and to seize it in its totality? One cannot win on every front! Simplification and panoramic views, therefore, are prerequisites.

***

The visual arts now enter into a new phase of creative turmoil (the third) relegating the former to the past. It consists of the elimination of representation (previously renewed and enriched—the aim now, however, is to supplant it).

A new landscape emerges: the great turning point being Ready-Made art, from which one has not yet recovered. Opponents of contemporary art consistently grab hold of it as an example, in their caustic criticism. It deserves, as a result, our fullest attention, whereas less emphasis will be placed on comparable parallel movements (such as collage or Action Painting, with which, in my opinion, it could be grouped).

It was Marcel Duchamp (1887-1968) who was responsible for this new surge. He had already drawn attention with his *Nu descendant un escalier*[8], inspired by Marey's chronophotographical lines (when set in space, time displays the speed of movement; this process also allows not to separate the moving body from its trajectory). He also distorted the female body, too, but the real reason why he created such a scandal was that his nude strolled about quite freely (walking down some stairs). Later, he elaborated original projects, based on automatism: runners, drums, rollers, staples; in short, a whole arsenal of machine-made objects invaded his work. But let us turn now to Ready-Made art, the source of so many disputes: a snow-shovel, a bottle rack, a urinal, a bike wheel attached to a kitchen chair, etc. Marcel Duchamp himself distinguished between "assisted ready-mades"—because he would often add a few words, or a graphic element lending more humour to the whole—and "reciprocal ready-mades," as for example the use of a Rembrandt—a copy—as an ironing-board.

(8) — *Nude descending a staircase* (Translators' note).

These examples are not to be taken, in my opinion, as mere craziness; if he is to avoid falling into academism, the artist is forced to invent, to renounce his acquired experience, so much so that to work one's way in this field is more and more difficult, now in particular, when everything has already been explored in every direction and saturation-point has almost been reached. As a result, plasticity develops in two separate stages. During the first period, the past is deconstructed and "liquidated," so to speak. All celebrated achievements are derided and destroyed, whilst there is nothing as yet with which to replace them. This stage—although blank in terms of its own output—enables a mustering up of energy; hence a sort of Dadaist frenzy, leading to a confused situation.

Ready-Made art is the best illustration of this stage of rejection: one must not, however, totally ignore its reverse side, which starts to emerge at this time.

It is true to say that Marcel Duchamp emphasized the provocative (or negative) side of his art: witness the urinal, the Gioconda sporting a moustache, or the coatstand nailed on the floor, which he called "*Trébuchet*" because the visitors to his workshop stumbled on it.[9] But its other aspect should not be overshadowed even despite, or rather by virtue of its relegation to the background. That which is concealed or minimized is of greater importance than that which is apparently on "exhibition."

Thanks to Ready-Made art, the machine-made object gains the status of a work of art in its own right. There are several reasons for this:

a) When exhibited in a museum or an art gallery, the bottle rack instantly loses its utilitarian aspect. When, some time later, a disciple, Man Ray, exhibits an iron on which he has stuck a line of nails, his purpose is really to show that it will no longer be of any use. The aim is precisely to impede the working of the object in order that what has hitherto remained in the dark may come under the spotlight.

Instruments which are considered humble because of their banality and their daily use (two causes of humiliation) reveal their real value which lies in their simple design and in a certain nobility, which they owe to this ultra-simplicity, this extreme soberness and to the total coherence of their morphology. The work of art, in this context, is that

(9) — A pun based on the fact that the pronunciation of the French "trébuchet" (an assay balance) is evocative of "trébucher," which means to stumble (Translators' note).

which dismisses fussiness, over-ornateness, "flashiness," and it even rules out all mystification as well as the celebration of well-worn compositions. For the aim is to free itself from the domination of naturalism and its repetitive motifs, such as floral shapes and lines.

However, it must not be concluded that Ready-Made art implies the praise of geometric art, constructivism, nor that of severe puritanism, of the reduction of domestic appliances to mere shells!

Rather it follows the opposite path to that of the Bauhaus: this school maintains that function gives rise to form, and in return that form depends solely on function ("less is more"). Ready-Made art on the other hand separates these two things; one must be kept at a distance in order that the other may become apparent and exist independently. An industrial object thus becomes a real work of art—an unprecedented occurrence (much to the dismay of the academy circles, those theorists defending unicity). And yet, every object is a "complex entity." Its richness should not be concealed, but extolled!

The object contains several strata: 1) the inside, the different parts, the motor, the belts; 2) the outside, the casing; 3) the visible parts by which to grip it, enabling its utilization: a pourer, a handle, a lever, better still, dials, keys, indicators; 4) its very components, the metal's brilliance, its colours, the choice of a material lacking in ornementation, which has not been inlaid (wood does not need to be grained; glass does not need to be engraved); 5) the organization of the parts and their interdependence: think of the watch, for instance; how have the watchcase, the hands, the straps, etc. been assembled and so firmly attached to each other?

The object is made up of so many different levels and plays so many different roles that it is impossible to predict what its final organization might be. Besides, it is preferable to ignore them because they place a barrier in front of the object. The aim is that from its multiple potentialities there emerges a new arrangement, which hitherto has been embedded and imprisoned in the object's unicity.

The desire for something new proves that this is not merely an anti-art, a form of derision, excentricity or revolt. These are but a means to an end, both caustic and essential, with which one destroys the prison in which our things, and we, ourselves, have been incarcerated.

b) Besides, reality may now generate works of art on its own, whereas they had been linked to deceptive representations and illusions: a revolution for which Ready-Made art is undoubtedly responsible. Consequently, it was the frame—generally rectangular in shape—, the picture of small size, Vasari's flat surface, and the habit of hanging things on the wall, which prevailed exclusively in museums. Now, however, the work is placed right in the middle of the room: it is "volumic," it cannot be ignored, it is sometimes gigantic, but whatever the case may be, it is always identical to that which it represents (the birdcage, the gas-burner, the coat-hanger). Thus, the gap has been bridged between the model and its reflection, and the two now coincide perfectly.

c) Furthermore—and confirming Ready-Made art's revolutionary status in the history of art—, the artist plays no part in the elaboration of the object, which has been found just as it is ("ready" is a word which characterizes our modern world of advertising, commerce and industry: hence phrases such as "ready-to-wear," "ready-to-eat," "ready for take-away," "ready-to-use," etc.)

Art has always been associated with the carrying out of certain processes and the battle against materials which resist one's efforts—such as the sculptor hewing stone, the ceramist mixing paste, the cabinet-maker carving wood, even the painter mixing his colours and applying them onto the canvas, etc.; this is the so-called aristotelian model, in which the hand and skill find great praise.

Here, there is nothing of the sort. The major activity is no longer creative, but conceptual; only the mind needs intervene in order to find the trick which will enable the "revelation" of the object (as in the case of the bottle rack).

Where is the novelty here? The chain-produced object, in its most utilitarian and prosaic form, becomes a "work of art" in its own right without having undergone any material transformation. Indeed, it is converted by an act of subversion.

On the other hand, as has already been mentioned, Marcel Duchamp generally associated several ready-mades (two, or more frequently even, three), in order to reach a happy medium: what better way than repetition to call uniqueness into question? Are goods not part of the world of quantity and series?

A prosaic and functional object which is deprived of its functional aspect; a real object and not merely a reflection; an object which has not been shaped nor perfected by a skilful craftsman: these three features are a good definition of the factory product, which has been "jazzed up" and has been given a new aesthetic character at the same time. It is now held in high esteem, even though one does not hesitate to manipulate it.

Negative attitudes—ridicule, provocation, caricature, humour—are inseparable from positive ones: the celebration of plasticity and of the modern world of machinery.

Thus, the gap is beginning to be bridged between art and automated construction: indeed, they tend to merge, as will be shown.

It is also time to reject—once and for all—the notion of the artist as a visionary (the inspired figure of romanticism), who laboriously conjures up—or so it goes—"a vision from elsewhere," something unparalleled, and remote from our industrialized world.

Man Ray—among many others—intensified and magnified this trend: he too applied himself to Ready-Made art, in each case, however, making additions to the object, thus destabilizing and transforming it.

Listed below are three known samples of these "objects of objects": those common objects which, thanks to a slight addition are suddenly renewed and given extra pathos:

1) "*Le Pain peint*[10]" (a pun which is generally successful): two sticks of bread are painted blue, producing surprise and amusement, as well as a sort of attraction on the audience (almost a magical transformation).

2) *It's Springtime*. Two bedstead springs are tied together in the middle so that they are crossed. The artist plays on the double meaning of the word "spring" and his only intervention consists in highlighting their opposition; plasticity is made more lively in this way.

3) *Obstruction*: all that is needed is a coatstand on which more coatstands are hung, until the effect is achieved of a migration of a flock of birds or of some strange congestion.

In short, the difference—which is tiny—between Duchamp and Ray is that the latter interferes slightly whereas the former not at all. This does not mean that Ray did not wish to explore the ready-made: after all, it was

(10) — "Painted bread." The comic effect is achieved thanks to the identical pronunciation of both terms in French (pain, peint). (Translators' note).

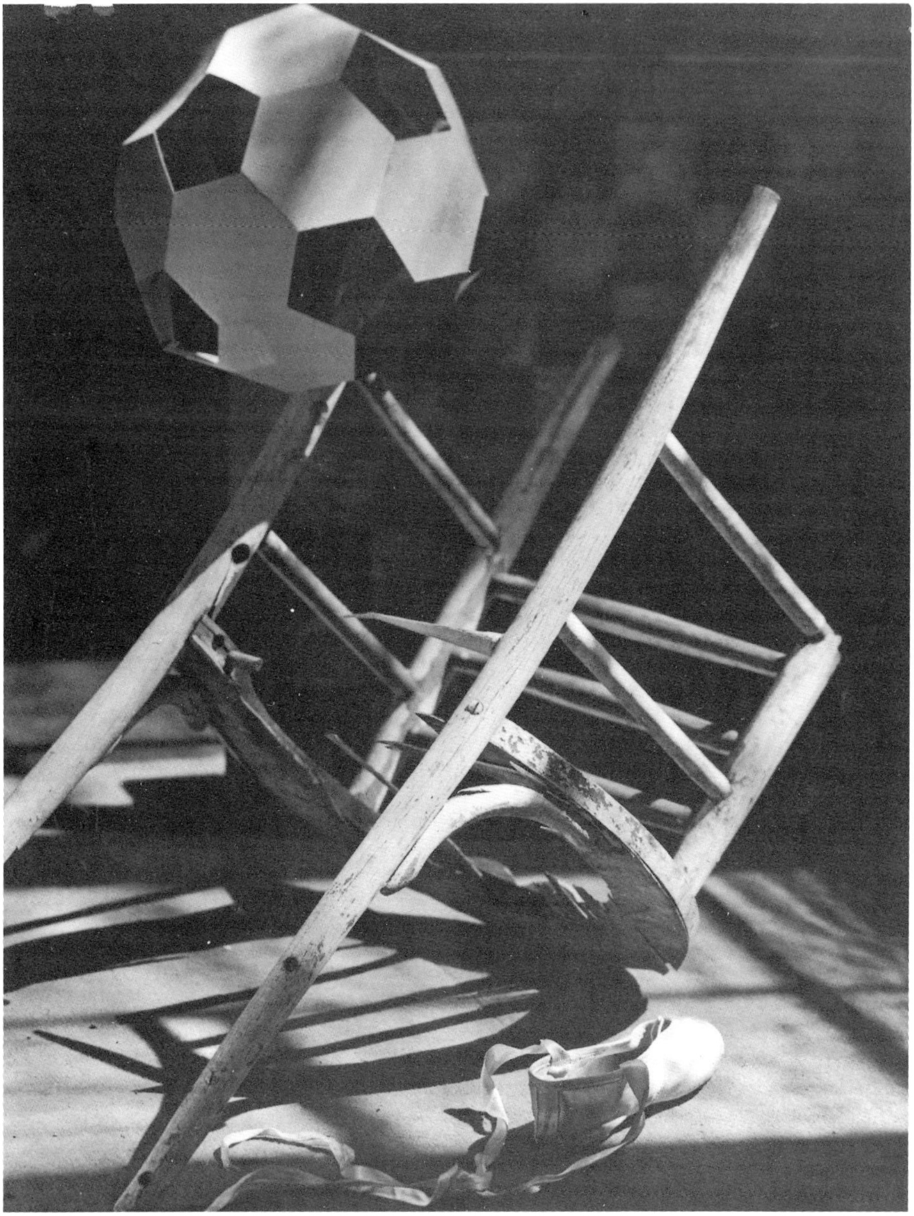

10 – Man Ray, *Objects*, 1932 (© by ADAGP, Paris 1992)
photo Musée National d'Art Moderne, Paris

he who invented the principle of "solarisation" (the "rayogramme," as he called it): an object is merely placed on a sheet of bromide paper in sunlight, and it leaves its atmospheric print.

No machinery, no effort is needed (in a word, the object, or whatever it may be, is "ready")! The emphasis, however, should fall on the essence of this remarkable form of art, on the fact that it can inhabit the most rudimentary or mechanized object (the coffee-grinder, the gas burner, the bottle rack). All they need is a little freedom in order to become expressive.

Ready-Made art will be discussed in further detail, for the way one judges it is a symptom of the way one understands the history of art. The ready-made is a sign, or rather the cause of a major change. It alters art in that the image of the object is replaced by the object itself (and frequently by the humblest of objects). At last, the object escapes from the canvas-prison and exhibits itself freely.

A few words must be added on Collage (contemporary with the ready-made), a famous artistic technique which also—although less violently—frees us from traditional pictoriality.

It emerged very slowly. The starting point was Picasso's and Braque's idea to copy a picture by Cézanne (*l'Evénement*), and to replace the newspaper which was depicted by a real newspaper. This was a skilful substitution—for he who gazes at the picture may not notice any difference—, and Picasso perfected the technique of deceptive picto-Collage: in his *Nature morte à la chaise cannée* (*Still Life with Cane Chair*, 1912), he even went so far as to simulate the seat cover by using a piece of oil cloth, the leafy pattern and the rings of which imitate the chair's canework. What a wonderful and bizarre mixture! We are being deceived by mere bits and pieces which cleverly replace that which was to be "represented."

It is easy to guess what the next step was: the generalization and the greater frequency of insertions, bearing no connection with the subject of the picture! Pieces of string, hair, sand, old underground tickets, fragments or broken pieces of anything at all are now placed on, or into the picture—the purpose being to redeem it from the lie it is propagating.

With no less authority, the world itself as a whole is summoned, is called into the stage of imagination.

And yet, what an ambivalent situation! On the one hand, these fragments are remarkable for their thinness: they even dissolve into the picture to which they add absolutely no relief. On the other hand, they cannot escape from their original function (simulation: they are the equivalent of what is normally painted). One cannot get away from a new kind of lie, which is incorporated in the larger one that is supposedly being denounced, but which is in fact strengthened. Only after a while will the Collage-pieces become noticeable, due to the lack of connection between them and the subject of the picture on which they are stuck. At the least, one perceives a superimposition, that an extra-layer has been added.

Let us now say a word or two about Action Painting, at the risk of anachronism. In traditional painting, three factors are required: the artist, the reality facing him, and the canvas; the first transposes the second onto the third.

In Action Painting, the second element is suddenly eliminated: the result is that the first now projects itself onto the third (which sometimes lies on the ground). He deposits onto it his transe-like states, his drives, his unleashed energy.

To a certain extent, the image or "representation" has not been fully discarded, but its constitutive energy is now made visible without the need of any intermediary. One is confronted with an "effect" rather than with a "reflection"—an effect, moreover, which cannot be separated from its cause. Thus, the action and its sequels (or its marks) are in complete concord—a perfect transposition is achieved, in which no altering or correcting technique has been used. The old lie already denounced by Plato long ago comes to an end: the risk of confusing reality and its double, an unsettling situation generating confusion (deception). From now onwards, the picture bears the mark of nothing which is not human or which is not the expression of man's fiery desires!

Finally, Ready-Made art, Collage, and Action Painting (pure gesture) renew the foundations of art. They call the whole system into question, with its machinery and tools. As regards Collage, scissors and glue have replaced paint brushes, and this is more obvious still in the case of Ready-Made art and Action Painting.

It is not enough to change one's "tools": the whole spirit of plasticity is being revolutionized. Art based on mirroring techniques comes to an end in the midst of this upheaval. Its very foundations have been shaken and its values, which have prevailed for centuries until now have lost all influence.

***

To restore to the object its rights or to rediscover it is only a first step, but in the final count, it is of negative value, given that it is a sign of protestation. Instead, it is more appropriate to celebrate it. But how? This signals the beginning of the fourth, the contemporary era.

Once "representation" has been worked on (the first stage of art); once it has undergone such original and magnificent renewal, where that which is left out by ordinary vision is included (the second stage, that of enrichment); and once an exit to the (saturated) system of figurative representation has been found, comes the positive stage of "presentation" (its apotheosis).

It is essential to be aware of these stages, as well as of the transitional periods. In this respect, an important transitional period was that which produced the empty space: both a paradoxical and fascinating situation, for the total absence of content appears to be the necessary condition for a "new" reality to follow later or for resubstantiation to occur. Anything that claimed to replace reality is dismissed.

Quite a few artists applied themselves to this task, resulting for instance in the translucence of the white square on a white background, verging on disappearance. At the risk of making an incongruous or even an unflattering comparison, it seems that this borderline experience and Ready-Made art share certain features: in its own way, the former also aims to abolish previous rules and to undermine evocative processes; the blank space stands in opposition to all lies.

But what vision of the object, the richness of which has been restored, does art offer, if not a revelation of an aspect hitherto unknown to one? If that were not the case, this art form would be assimilated with documentary-making!

Without claiming to exhaust the problem, let us take a look at three possible answers to it: those of Christo, Arman and Dubuffet. The aim is simply to throw light onto the "spirit" in which they go about solving the problem, onto the underlying logic which dictates their creativity.

But why choose these three? Why leave out Buren, Viallat or Hantaï and so many others? Is this not the sign again of arbitrariness and bias? The answer is that those who have not been included in the demonstration would also agree with the present thesis. Furthermore, the choice of which artist to use as an illustration is made in view of purely didactic reasons: they are the best examples, showing in what way the renewal of the object has come to the foreground.

Everyone knows that in 1985, Christo—with whom will be dealt at greater length than the two others—wrapped up the Pont Neuf in Paris. This achievement alone contains sufficient significance for one to question its true meaning and to have enough in one's plate. Besides the bridge, he has also sheeted over remparts, castles, museums, even mountains and shores.

Man Ray had already, when making slight additions to his ready-mades, used wrapping techniques in his arrangements. His wrapped and tied "sewing machine" is one of the best known examples. It is entitled "Isidore Ducasse's Enigma," echoing that which the surrealist Ducasse had achieved, or at least advocated: the chance encounter of "a sewing machine and an umbrella on a dissection table."

Man Ray, whose speciality was to play games with his audience, meant to increase the bizarreness and mysteriousness of this cacophonous assembly (a Dadaist method) by introducing a covering sheet.

The same gesture might appear to point to the same achievement. And yet, the great similarity between the two packaging techniques does not exclude a major difference—such that it is pointless to try to put them together or to compare them.

The intention (which counts the most in modern art) is not the same. On the one hand, one unsettles and creates something strange (a negative force which undermines the object's identity), and on the other hand, by means of an apparent enclosure, one seeks to pave the way for a new adventure, to set things free. So, the two paths do not meet.

Furthermore, it is also significant that Christo will happily wrap even the gigantic (a mountain, the sea, a town), whereas Man Ray does not apply himself to anything of beyond ordinary proportions. This confrontation within the Immense confirms the gap, and stops one from drawing parallels between the two.

Can Christo really be classified as an artist? The answer is most definitely: "yes!". Granted it is no longer painting but urban experiments or Land Art. Nonetheless, even though his art is ephemeral—for he soon unwraps that which he has wrapped—, he does not fail to photograph or to reword these wrappings in different ways, and then exhibits or commercializes them in the normal way.

This transient "camouflaging" has attracted different interpretations, such as that his work is an attempt to evoke resurrection. Christo Javachev has discarded his name and kept only his Christian name, with its Christian resonance precisely. Is he not exploiting our collective imagination around the shroud, the embalming and the entombment in order to suggest with greater forcefulness a time of return and rebirth? The act of "veiling" and of "unveiling" would, according to this interpretation, express a religious victory over death, hence the subsequent reappearance—or emergence—of that which had disappeared.

Other interpretations, which do not necessarily exclude this one, can be sought:

1) Instead of painting the universe onto the canvas, and hanging it up on the wall, the reverse takes place: the universe is enclosed in a canvas-veil. The former is no longer on the latter's surface, rather the latter abolishes and contains the former. In the past, the immense universe was projected onto a screen where it shone brightly: now the envelope is avenged and supplants what it is used to support.

An artist, in my opinion, is someone who is able to find a new approach to reality and who establishes a new relationship with it; someone who is able to give rise to both a physical and a metaphysical experience, and even, at times, as in the present case, to a "borderline experience."

The true artist attracts attention to himself not only because of the changes he has made, but also because he has totally transformed the act of painting (the world is no longer copied in small format onto the canvas; it is the canvas which contains and is wrapped around the world).

Other similar techniques include: painting a canvas onto the canvas, in other words painting its micro-relief, its strange texture; tearing it (either the canvas is effectively lacerated or else a torn canvas is painted onto a canvas which is intact, adding to the unsettling effect) so that it reveals its thickness and its underlying layers.

It goes without saying that paint brushes and colours are made redundant: the enclosing white cloth (sheet) is all that is needed, which is not surprising.

2) Another interpretation is that Christo's achievement is an attempt to erase precisely that which cannot be ignored, such as barricades, walls, shores, hills, etc. What calls more attention than a bridge which by uniting a city's sides increases its size?

It is a fact, however, that our world all too often resorts to demarcations, bridges and towers. Constant battles have been fought around border issues. The drive to possess requires landmarks, tangible borders and crossing points (buildings, roads, anything which calls attention).

By wrapping these up, he lifts the "anchors": the world, no longer divided but homogeneous, is liberated. All intrusive forms—natural or urban—are effaced in order to level out the universe. The differences are restored only after a mere eclipse, but the moment in which theses things were abolished remains engraved in memory.

3) These interpretations may give an insight into Christo's work; it would seem preferable, however, to place the emphasis on the stratagem of packaging itself: on both its importance and its novelty. For to wrap something up also signifies that mountain, river or shore, by definition impossible to grasp by hand, are being subjected to the same norms as our utensils (as if both indiscriminately should be transported and immobilized).

In commerce, great importance is given to the outer-layer of the goods. They are never offered as such: their value must be enhanced, a minimal effort at least must be made in their presentation (first, their display—in the shop-window, on the shelf, or if it is hung up) and still more in the different ways they might be packaged and protected (tin, bottle, bag, case, cartridge or box). Thanks to its "dressing," the object is singularized, and the usual reproaches—namely that it is simple and standardized—no longer apply. In order to protect it, one even sometimes goes to the length of placing it in a casket or in a gangue.

In nature too, the outer appearance which conditions and enhances the inside is exploited to increase the value of whatever it may be; the outer surfaces are shinier than that which they enclose. Take fruit for example: it is contained in a close capsule which compresses it, whilst also sculpting and protecting it—the orange peel, the pea pod, the skin of the grape or the shiny one of the apple, etc. Man dresses too, and skin continues to provide him with a flexible coating; for once, let us steal the spontaneous principle of fruit or man: let us enclose or wrap up!

In this way, things recover some of their relief. The Pont Neuf, for example, has recovered some of its originality. Given that our cities are hyper-functional, the idea is to make the use of certain things difficult so that reality may astound us once more. Resorting to a "wrapping-unwrapping" process seems to be one of the most effective methods of achieving this. It would be wrong to see in this process a kind of sequestration of the object, its caging or its burial, for the artist aims at the exact opposite result.

Christo is aware of this: "Rodin made a nude sculpture of Balzac. He found him fat, flabby and ugly, so he covered him up, and in so doing, turned the statue into a masterpiece. And generally speaking, it is the case that when one covers or wraps something up, it is sublimated. The point is that by wrapping up an object, one gives rise to an emotion.[11]"

The essential thing, in my opinion, is that the monument has gained something in being wrapped up: it is as if attention has been focused on it; it is ready for birth and for rebirth. The display gives rise to a real anamorphosis, or a re-creation.

Less time will be spent on the other two artists, Arman and Dubuffet, although, if one were thorough in one's approach, one ought to analyse their methods in greater depth.

Amongst other surprising strategies, Arman systematically adopts that of accumulation, or else he simply stacks things in heaps.

"Often an object stops being an object when multiplied": this affirmation by Arman is the key to his innovative method (which is a real discovery). Indeed, when you see a single orange or a single Coca Cola can (the same goes for a comb or a door-knob), the former appeals to your hunger and the latter to your thirst (demonstrating the instinct which comes into play, the appeal to refreshment, a comestible object).

(11) — Christo, le Packaging, in *Dynasteurs*, October 1986, p. 58.

But when oranges are grouped on a display shelf or in a shop window, or when boxes are piled on top of each other, these objects, by definition, due to their great number, no longer refer you to thirst or to hunger: the abundance of objects exceeds your desire for them and reveals what has hitherto remained in the dark: the object's unnoticed morphology or an original assembly of pieces.

In short, the quantity of functional objects kills their very functionalism or, to put it differently, the adding together of identical things results in a new configuration, in a strange and stupefying heap. Furthermore, as pointed out by Arman, repetition is always castigated: but when it takes on such intensity, it gives rise to a mutation, to an explosion.

Essentially, a seemingly basic operation has enabled the "transfiguration" to take place. Even the most commonplace object comes out of it differently and gains a more noble nature.

Following on from embalming and accumulation, let us consider another experimental method, both an exploration and a revelation of an unknown aspect of the inexhaustible object. It is taken from Dubuffet's first period (1953), an artist who will be discussed again later, when I come to deal with the evolution of tendencies in contemporary art. Need it be said that it is impossible at this point to establish a deciding-line between yesterday's and today's art? The two merge into each other. Each perspective amplifies, widens and abolishes the limits of the other, so that any given artist marks the end of an era at the same time as he initiates a new one.

Dubuffet zealously picks up objects which are deteriorating in one way or another, or rotting, those whose past splendor has faded: rubbish of all kinds, dried leaves which are starting to fritter away, sweepings, dust, and sand in particular... He wets them, crushes them, and after having ground them, he makes a sort of gruel out of them which he then spreads onto a hard plate. The result is an extremely thin layer. Ink is then applied uniformly; after which, he spreads onto this apparently lifeless surface (given its destruction through vigorous mixing) a sheet of "good paper," chosen for its absorbability (smooth and made up with lots of glue): it may thus become impregnated by a paradoxically "burgeoning" matter which has been pulverized (submitted to torture).

It should be noted in passing that the artist works in a laboratory.

The result is not so much a picture but a high-relief plank on which are exhibited the prints of reality as well as the minute traces of its turbulence.

Thus, even the object which has been demolished continues to contain movement and vibrant life. "I like to claim that my art is an attempt to rehabilitate that which is decried [...] The different voices of dust, its soul—these interest me much more than the flower, the tree or the horse, for I sense that they are far *stranger*. Dust is a being so different from ourselves.[12]"

Reality, that which escapes our vision, is made up of different layers: the most obvious, the macroscopic, the one which absorbs our whole attention, hiding the others from us. The artist's task is to throw light on all of these! It is his task to unravel from the squashed object that which it contains!

The field of study has not changed: placed before us is still an object. It has merely changed dimensions and become miniaturized.

***

The present analysis has concentrated on three merely technical processes (but what is art, if not the poetizing of technical processes?) enabling the modification, the unravelling and the renewal of the object. The last of these even went so far as to attempt the erasure of all remnants of form (considered to be a carapace which serves to conceal), in order that a more discreet, buried and therefore imperceptible life may come to the fore. The aim is to destroy the object's old defence system. Embalming it renews it (through rebirth); its multiplication, by virtue of proliferation alone, opens up a new perspective; sheer number is guaranteed to drown an all-too absorbing functionalist view of the object.

The intention was not to list all the resources available to art. It is sufficient to have pointed out a few of those which prove capable of fulfilling its subversive mission: the perpetual "de-simplification" of objectivity.

(12) — Jean Dubuffet, *l'Homme du commun à l'ouvrage*, Idées/Gallimard, Paris, 1973, p. 230

CHAPTER III

Art's move towards the object

Given the historical evolution of art, the following thesis seems inevitable, although somewhat surprising in itself: namely that the work of art, which has been overestimated and viewed through the eyes of a romantic philosophy, which cultivates pathos whilst at the same time carefully keeping secret its methods or its creational principles, is being replaced by something different.

And yet, Valéry had warned against and denounced this kind of mystification: the only thing to which he attributed any importance for the poet (from the Greek *poiein*, to create) was the act of "doing."

More to the point, the artist has become a physicist who investigates quality (scientists have long lost interest in the different sorts of grain, paste, texture and earthy substances), and he is concerned precisely with the exploration of the elements' hidden possibilities, with daring mixtures, or even with the organization of various elements (the art of installation-works, which corresponds to his morphogenetic passion). If one wanted to use a risky term, one might compare him to an alchemist. "Experimenter" seems more appropriate, though, and it is this vision of the artist that I shall try to defend and to illustrate as well.

Indeed, not very long ago, the plastician's work-methods were comparable to those of the craftsman, who manipulates substances (Dubuffet himself refused to make the distinction between the artistic painter and the house painter). Contemporary artists however, in my opinion,work according to methods used in the factory, just like the engineer. The novelty is that the model based on manual work has given way to one based on mechanization or machine-production. This does not imply that the creator has become the advocate, or the follower of a society which is only interested in trade and productivity; he simply mimics its processes, and steals its enriching secrets.

It must be stressed that solely plasticism and the path in which it has embarked is being considered in the present argument. But the aim is not to deny nor to underrate the toiling existence of all those who continue in their "theoretical practice," those who work in the margin, or those who would rather give free rein to psyche's fantasy world, to the dramas of their unconscious (a personal, projective and subjective painting, at a time when the romantic ego is in obvious decline)—far from it! These fields from the past may still give rise to surprising developments, but this is no reason for ignoring the newest techniques, which are directed towards "sculpture-painting" or "object-art."

The rather paradoxical idea that abstract art paved the way or anticipated this new art form is not to be dismissed; it embarked on an endless mission which was to sound out the object. Instead, however, of becoming fascinated to the exclusion of all else by the splendour of particular things as does figurative art (each apple is different from the next), its aim is to afford one to delight in universality (the structure of things in themselves), and in a less appearance-based dynamic world.

Nevertheless, this kind of art also has its faults: it gives pride of place to geometry and it remains at a level of generalization such that the almost sensual appreciation one expects when in contact with a work of art is frustrated (vision has too much precedence over touch); finally and above all, like it or not, it becomes assimilated into the representational system. This was the most stubborn obstacle in the way of the contemporary revolution. Before it could be achieved, iconoclastic manoeuvering was needed such as Ready-Made art, Collage, and even Action Painting.

Only then did a kind of interior architecture become possible, whereby art entered into effective achievements. I shall show later that this trend intersected with another, which was more or less unrelated to it, and was reinforced by it: the products of daily life met with the method which enabled them to free themselves from their century-old prison and which totally transformed them. It was no longer impossible to find beauty in the street, inside houses and inhabiting the most commonplace objects, since it was one of its aims to bring the old elitist segregation to an end.

The two movements intersect: one is dedicated to extolling the object in its complete and inexhaustible three-dimensionality in almost religious terms; the other frees the trivial object from its functionalist prison (design). One works its way from above, the other from below, and they meet in the middle. Each will be analysed in term, before I look at their fusion. Both go towards making up the "object-art."

***

It would be proper to start by mentioning and interpreting an important trend—as well as an ambiguous one, namely Pop Art, which evolved mainly in the most advanced part of American society [1].

Pop Art seems to confirm the view that an aesthetics has emerged which is both industrialized and industrial: industrialized because it readily considers the work of art a commodity just like any other, which can even be sliced up and sold; industrial because it has undoubtedly borrowed its stereotypes and modes of execution from the manufacturing society (moulding, serial-production, transferring, etc.). It might well be, then, that the intention behind the imitation is derogatory and has a deconstructive purpose. This point will need further examination.

Certainly, it is very noticeable that in most cases, Pop Art applies itself to photomontage, advertisements and to representational games: it puts forward uniform, garish "surfaces," so to speak strips devoid of depth and shadow, so that the present theory is no longer valid, or so it seems.

However, some artists unhesitatingly turn away from these "images" and concern themselves with environmental works (for instance a cake bigger than the skyscrapers between which it is hung).

The advertising poster may also be regarded as an object from two points of view: on the one hand, because of its dimensions (its large size);

(1) — The phrase "popular art" is said to have been coined in London, as early as 1955. At this time, it referred to the work done in the wake of Schwitters. The latter, taking collage to its logical conclusion, had come up with the idea of sticking residue together, such as cork slices and bits of material or paper. Picabia's influence, seen from a surrealist angle and taking into account the surprise provoked by its devices, should not be overlooked. Later on, Pop artists made piles of boxes, cans, pans, springs, etc., thus evoking a bazar.

Here, I must admit to a slight hindrance for the rest of the argument. I have already used the works of Vasarely, Arman, César, Viallat, Hantaï, etc. in previous books. Having already taken them as examples, I cannot do so again. I will nonetheless allude to Jean Dubuffet *in fine*.

on the other, because it displays common, everyday life appliances or products, sometimes reproduced with outstanding accuracy (a sort of derisive pseudo-advertising: a packet of washing powder, a can of soup, a car tyre).

Lichtenstein goes even further: he devotes himself to plaster sculpture and ceramics, onto which he nonetheless roughly sketches lines, grooves and a whole host of dots. Is the intention humorous or decorative? The answer is: it is neither! "My aim, he said, was to place two-dimensional symbols onto a three-dimensional object." What a reversal! Contrary to classical art—which is being attacked on all sides—and which aimed to convey the illusion of volume (the three dimensions) on an even canvas, signs of flatness are now projected onto a relief.

Besides, it is interesting that a number of the major american Pop artists first worked as window dressers (hence what we have called the art of installation works, if not of display windows), or in advertising. Consequently, Pop Art has always been linked to the world of shops, of consumption, of montage; although painting, rather than the object, seems to be its first priority, it remains that the latter is a major concern of the former, which it overwhelms (repetition, accumulation, illusions).

There remains a last doubt of which Pop Art still needs to be cleared: either it is inspired by a merely satiric and caustic point of view, and its purpose is to bring about the demise of the industrial system—this would be the dark or the negative side that is characteristic of any ironical attitude—, or it contributes to glorify urban culture, taking it to the extreme and celebrates prosaic things: a fan, a cooker, a street lamp, a coat hanger, etc. If the second hypothesis is true, Pop Art must be considered a live branch of today's art, and as such, a place must be found for it on the great map of contemporary original achievements. But where?

Another good reason for paying special attention to Pop Art is that it seems to combine the two trends already mentioned spontaneously: it can be considered a sort of montage, and at the same time, it incorporates elements of everyday life: a packet of washing powder, a tube of toothpaste... Could it be that we have already stumbled upon the eagerly awaited art form which celebrates a combination of trends? If such were the case, Pop Art would be a very important reconciliation factor. This is a point that must be decided on.

A fairly widespread misconception must also be corrected: the emergence of Pop Art was a necessity, given that it was born and developed in different places, and at different times; so that, although it flourished in the United States, it must not be seen as a strictly American movement.

It first occurred in Europe: indeed, Picasso's astoundingly hyperrealistic *Assiette aux gaufrettes* dates back to as early as 1914. And in 1941, he had already carved a wooden cigar and put it on a matchbox. But it really took off in England (in around 1950), with the *Independent Group*. These artists—Phillips, Hamilton, Hockney, Blake, Smith and Kitaj too—exploited the means of their time: photography, magazines, postcards, films, posters. They deliberately rejected any kind of subtlety, and refused to separate art from life. This was the birth of Pop Art, which was linked from the start to the environment and to mass-produced goods.

As a rule, Pop Art provides us with the highest degree of banality: a Coca-Cola can, a packet of cigarettes, a tyre, a cooker, a ball of string, a film star in front of the mirror, a tennis racket, etc. The aim is merely to reproduce the commercial system. Should Warhol, Lichtenstein, Rosenquist and their fellow artists be counted amongst the favoured few, the objectographs or the "objectors" of the future, those who revolutionized contemporary art?

What are their work methods? What is being expressed by way of an apparent hyper realism, which is so different from former tendencies—consisting in refinements of a European kind, in abstract geometrism, or in Action Painting, with all the excitement it brings with it?

The artist now deliberately appeals to typically mechanical processes to produce his "work": a series of panels placed side by side, or identical photographs endlessly reproduced (several Giocondas are better than just one, he adds most impertinently). The gallery in which the works are exhibited may sell "little bits" or fragments of them; but was it not already previously the case that a lone hand of a statue was enough to entrance the archeologist and art amateur?

In some cases, artists use stencils or else, they simply take commercial posters which they might assemble or combine, the main aim being to paint the gaps in between.

This form of art leads to the poorest, the coldest, the most imper-

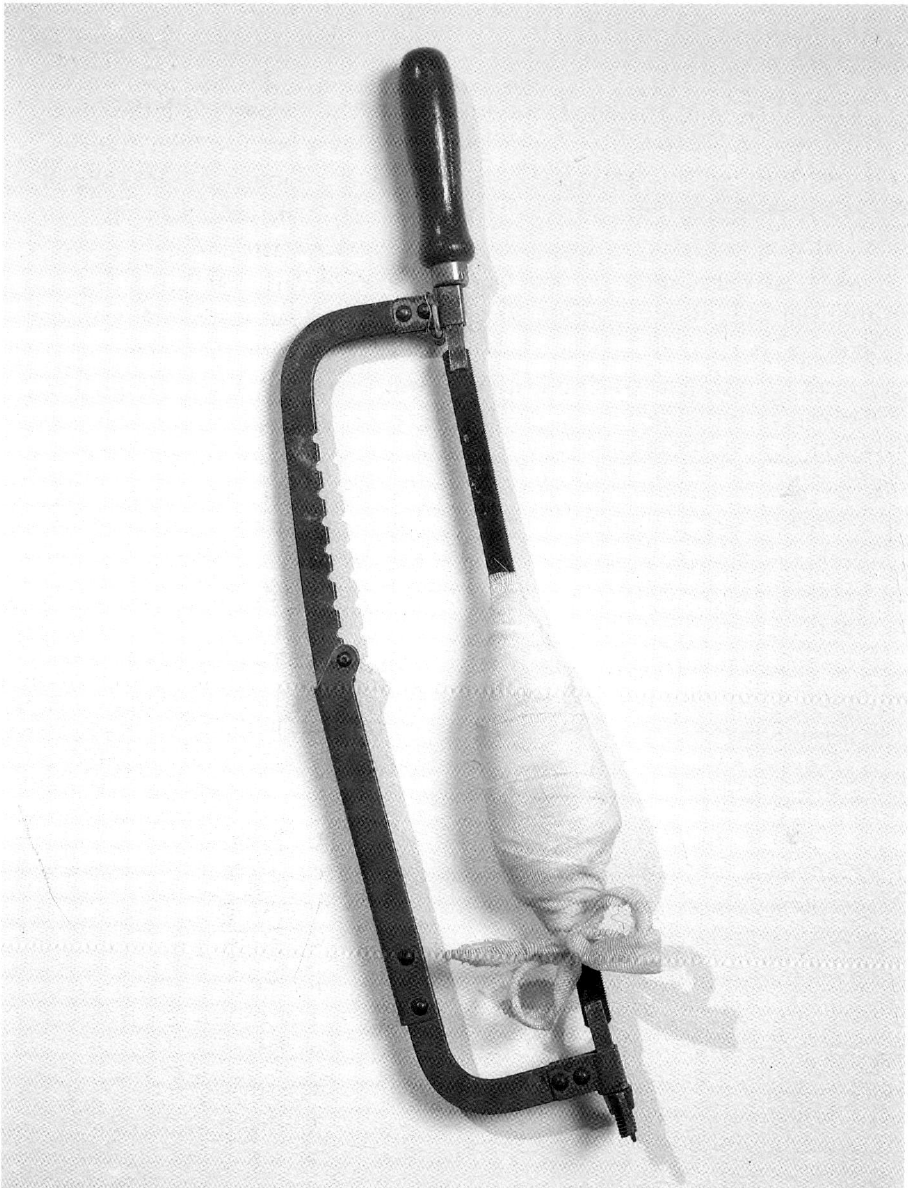

11 – Erik Dietman, *Sick Saw*, 1960/61
photo Galerie Claudine Papillon, Paris

sonal imagery, as well as the most banal: the soup can is made to glitter and look new, implying that it has not been used; because if it had, functionality would prevail over its double which would thus be depreciated; it is obvious that these artists are inspired by commercial art, which only displays brand new and glossy goods. Lacquered, chromium-plated, or metallic substances, even neon or crude lighting are extolled by this "Pepsi art," or "Pampryl art[2]," as some cynical critics have called it.

Besides, it is very difficult to describe this art form since it has assimilated so many "clever tricks" borrowed from all sides: it might be less simple or less commonplace than some people think, for it incorporates many innovations from other movements, and magnifies or exaggerates them.

For instance, it threw itself into "gigantism": a hamburger, two meters high and wide, or a piece of cake so huge that it is taller than the buildings between which it is placed.

This is no minor matter (nor is it a secondary consideration): this alone has led to a revolution in painting, at least in classical painting, which implied a frame and small format—a narrow window, a sort of skylight, from where the world was observed.

Fresco painting already distances itself from the picture and calls into question the "enemy," representation; this is the first step into the world of objects, with all it implies: its obstructiveness, its immensity, and hence the difficulties in finding a place for it since it may be too large to be exhibited in a museum.

Let us briefly mention that a certain American plastician once needed several helicopters in the execution of his art: two were used to stretch out the canvas, while the aerial artist stood on a sort of platform, and threw a stream of acrylic paint onto it!

Action Painting was the first to go down this path, although it did so rather hesitatingly. It is well known that Pollock would dance on large canvases which were spread on the ground. Monet (*les Nympheas*[3]) and Picasso (*Guernica*) also produced (relatively) monumental works, although this was the result of a process of enlargement rather than a deliberate choice to put forward something of colossal dimensions.

(2) — Pampryl is a brand of fruit juice (Translators' note)
(3) — *Water-Lilies* (Translators' note)

In order to achieve such gigantic (and difficult) works, the artist must often associate pieces of equal size (placing them side by side, in the same way as blocks of plaster are stuck together in building): the same element is repeated over and over again, and the whole becomes part of the environment.

However, there are many different variations on the theme of endless repetition: Rosenquist, for instance, remains with a canvas of traditional size, but he only paints a tiny detail on it: a shirt collar, a finger, a waistcoat... thus leaving the spectator with the task of integrating them into a whole and of discovering the immensity which has only been suggested through the subtle use of selection.

It should also be noted that all contemporary artists, whatever the school to which they belong, have been driven to execute works of monumental proportions, often as one form or another of protest and varying in their inventiveness (Dubuffet, César, Vasarely...). But none have matched Pop Art's rivalry with skyscrapers and its invasion of the city.

Pop Art also invented another "trick," namely the superimposition of two surfaces; as some critics have pointed out, this was merely the application of the "and/or" technique.

What is being suggested when the easily identifiable American flag is coated with some substance, or when it is covered with blotches of paint? It becomes both a symbol and a medley of colours, intended to unsettle the spectator.

A similar device was to re-use the widespread technique of "inclusion," whereby fragments of reality (bits of cardboard, or pieces of broken plate...) are mixed into the paste.

But this sort of "super-collage" intended to undermine illusion and deceptive imitation is not new. Modern art, with its renowned leap out of two-dimensionality and its comforting leap back into a reality from which art had become remote, has often both preached and practised this technique, as we all know. Pop Art, however, has given it a very original touch by including real tools within the canvas or the montage: a radio set which has been switched on, a ringing alarm clock, or even, in Rauschenberg's *Winter Pool* (1959), a ladder placed between the two parts of a huge diptych.

All these methods—gigantism, inclusion of fragments or of goods, serial repetition, the use of two-dimensional commercial art or of road signals, the choice of extremely banal images, including those of work clothes or of food for instance—demonstrate the vitality and the daring of the American movement, but they also show that it has been inspired by urban society, by the megalopolis and by consumerism.

In a way, this aesthetics resembles that of Precisionist painters who did not omit any detail in the scenes they reproduced and accentuated their tendency to concentrate on everyday life by "re-duplicating" commonplace goods and by depicting them with great accuracy, as though they were trying to give rise to confusion (making it impossible to distinguish the image from the original). However, Pop Art is not interested in this kind of optical realism, in reaching absolute similarity or exact identification, and does not seem to be at all concerned by the meticulous reproduction of details (the "niggling stroke" technique).

In order to get a better idea of this movement, let us stop and consider one of its famous achievements for a while: Lichtenstein's *Young Girl Looking at herself in a Mirror* (1964).

The plastician introduces the mirror not to imitate traditional art (the self-portrait), but to play with duplicating processes, exact replica, and trompe-l'oeil iconography. He applies himself to produce an effect of indetermination (which seems more real: the young girl or her reflection?).

More curiously still, the girl looking at herself sees herself as being made up of a haze of infinite dots, evoking the frame of a television screen, or of a comic strip; as a consequence, this image is less an image than the image of an image!

Not only is she depicted as a seedbed of dots, but even the hand holding the mirror is caught in the same network, which goes to prove the all-engulfing nature of this process. It has now become impossible for any one to separate "reality" from its double: both are equally caught up in the web of this reticular mechanism.

It is perfectly obvious that the portrait (very similar to a comic strip) is schematized and over-simplified and that it is totally laminated. As Lichtenstein noted, this was a way to oppose the impastoed painting which was in fashion in Europe at the time: hence the preference given to the new American texture, consisting in dots and thin layers.

Not very long ago, two components were needed to produce a work,

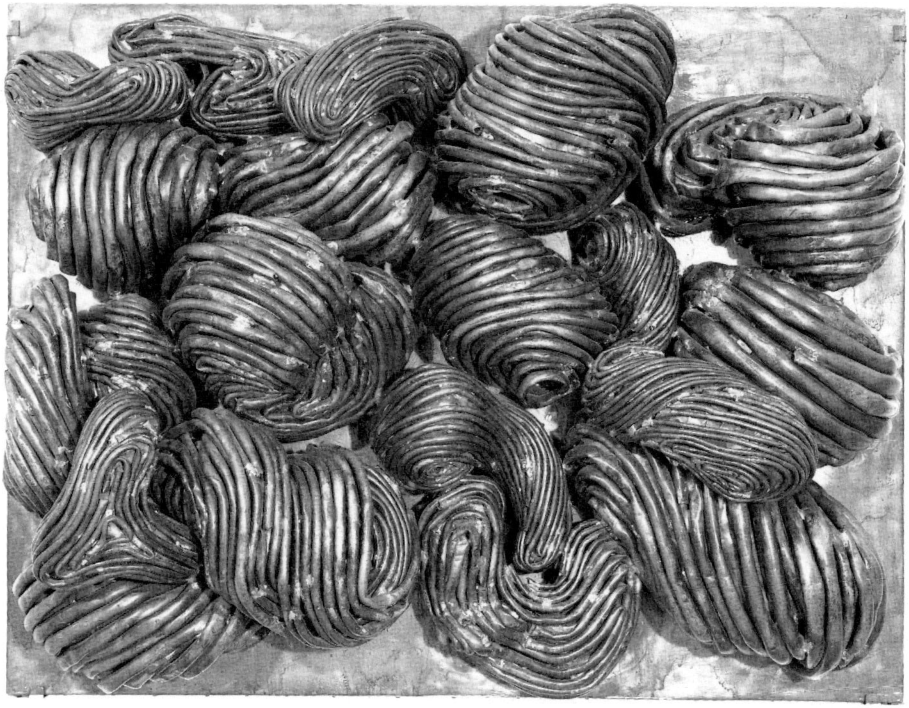

12 – Zoltan Kemeny, *Thought treated as Form*, 1962
photo Musée National d'Art Moderne, Paris

the artist and that which he represented (the image). A third actor has now come between them, and threatens to replace both of them: the image of the image (the poster, the shop- or road-sign, the illustration).

Reality has been abolished in favour of stereotypes; the world grows more and more unreal. Beings of flesh and blood are being replaced by photographs, which are in turn processed by a duplicating industry, by the flood of advertising, with its typography, its programming, the specific texture of its images. Under these circumstances, painting Coca-Cola cans, or Campbell's soup-cans does not express a concern for the complex object; on the contrary, it is to be seen as a caustic denunciation or protest against the tendency to move away from the world, to impoverish it and to replace it by signs that can be easily manipulated. The aim is not to present us with an image of our civilization, but rather with a civilization dominated by the omnipotent image.

Pop Art thus belongs to the (classical) trend which condemns both machines and goods. The United States were all the more prone to welcome it as this puritan society blames consumption and the overwhelming advertising which induces one to buy Pop Art even makes use of what it disapproves in order to organize its crusade: deception, repetition, cold impersonality; it deliberately brandishes that which is most common and most widely used, for instance a packet of cigarettes, a car tyre, a coat hanger, etc.

For all this, it is not a list of goods one would find in a shop catalogue, for it is their very insignificance which is stressed.

One of the main purposes of Pop Art is to expose the media's tyranny over us, and it does this by means of a parodic aesthetics: by showing up certain stereotypes, it must make us see that we are totally surrounded by stereotypes. Nonetheless, there are a few apparent exceptions to this rule.

For instance, when Warhol exhibits a Campbell's soup can with torn and damaged labels (tragic Pop Art?), is this the sign of a change, has he turned away from brand new and glossy objects? If rusty and ragged items come to appear in the foreground, then, it seems that Pop Art's strategy is no longer effective since it no longer emphasizes the power of poster images to deceive.

However, that such a change really does occur is questionable: the aim is not to signify the death of the image, but to shift the emphasis so that the image now appear as an instrument of death. And it may be considered this way from two points of view. On the one hand, the image had already overcome and set aside the real world: in its repetitiveness, coldness, dullness, it was a symbol already of enslavement and destruction; on the other hand, the change initiated by Warhol makes its function quite obvious: the image is being gnawed away by its own annihilating power. No real change has taken place, the same process has simply become more intense.

It seems that the celebration of goods is Pop Art's way to deny them: it makes as if it embraced and clasped them in its arms, only to better suffocate them after. Under the guise of a realistic art, it cleverly undermines that which it portrays.

Let us add that contemporary art has grown more complex: it often includes two different stages (first, to criticize the old rules and to destroy them, and then to reconstruct). Pop Art certainly belongs to the first stage (deconstruction). Later will come a time for a more satisfactory task, less bitter and closer to a real celebration.

Admittedly, until now, "negative" or critical attitudes have often prevailed, as in the case of Ready-Made art. For much energy is needed to stop the old order from extending into the present. The artist's task, then, is limited to adopting a derisive or destructive attitude. The emergence of a positive attitude, on the other hand, is more difficult to achieve. Once he has freed himself, the artist is at last able to lead us into the core of an endless, unfathomable, and always unknown reality.

So Pop Art, bogged down in consumer goods, belongs to the time of harsh criticism and ironic distance, making use of duplication in particular (the "déjà vu," which is either enlarged or simplified). All in all, the core of this painting remains the object, often broken but always omnipresent; and if it is not the object, its double has taken its place (something garish, enamelled and glossy, the purpose of which is to create panic and confusion).

***

I would readily agree with a contemporary critic, Jean-Clarence Lambert, who acknowledges four possibilities for modern plasticians: "Artists have on the whole followed four methods. The first is to "de-realize" their work [...] The second [...] is to render enigmatic [...] The third is to have recourse to dramatization [...] And finally, quantitative methods come into play: accumulation, "serialization," and other manipulations[4]." Other methods could certainly be included, especially innovating practices ("working ideas," as Frank Stella put it) which enhance and enrich the object.

It is always easier to start by deprecating that which has gone before : Pop Art brilliantly succeeded in this, so brilliantly that it seemed ambiguous to some, as though it were hesitating between commercial realism on the one hand and icy mockery on the other, having fun and taking delight in exaggerating deceptive devices. Tinguely's experience could be interpreted as being in the same vein.

Tinguely openly rejected painting because he felt that it had become completely ossified. Besides, how does one decide to stop painting? "I never knew when to stop, he said. I could go on with a painting for months, scraping off, painting over, and before the paint could even dry starting all over again... It is this situation that brought the idea of motion to my mind. Motion simply allowed me to avoid becoming ossified in my turn[5]."

Consequently, he replaces painting, which is no longer possible—and its brushes, its palette, its frame, and its easel—with old iron and all possible sorts of scrap, sheet metal, girders, wire-strainers, rails, straps, track rods, wires, tubes, anything one might find in a flea-market (or in a waste-container). He twists, entangles and connects them all: thanks to an electric circuit which is carefully hidden, the baroque machinery is set in motion (a device very different from Calder's, who only relied on the trembling brought by the air or by the slightest breeze). Tinguely's automata revolve, stop and start again, whilst at the same time setting off musical instruments, flashes of light or fireworks.

After having produced all this noise and excitement, the system falls apart and breaks down—but only to start up once more after this slightly worrying interruption, with a few initial convulsions and "clinging" sounds.

Here, our machines are being held in high esteem and being derided at

(4) — Jean-Clarence Lambert, *le Parti-pris des objets*, "Opus", April 1969, p. 75.
(5) — Interview from June 1976.

the same time (the machine is shown to "commit suicide"!). Tinguely confesses to having mainly cultivated "the machine's crazy, auto-destructive, repetitive playful side, the sisyphian trap which forces it to come and go in the same direction."

In spite of all his original features, Tinguely provides insights which are helpful in the present analysis: he became a sort of mechanic and thought of himself as a "constructivist," as a champion for (Dadaist) automated constructions, nonetheless prone to madness and absurdity.

Let us add two general remarks in passing:

a) In the long run, the plastician becomes bored with his playful and vitriolic practice: soon he might turn to "sanctifying" the object, for "celebration" is indeed the real artist's aspiration.

b) Moreover, the only true criterion for a plastic artist is whether or not he has managed to "transform" past practices or even his own ones (he must be a "dabbler").

To return to Jean-Claude Lambert's panoramic description, it has now been fully established that art may contain a gratingly ironical intention, that it may be based on the attack of and contempt for the object. In some cases however, there is reason to cast some doubt: is the object truly under attack and fire? When Christo packages the Pont-Neuf, various monuments, cities, landscapes, does he intend to bury them, to hide them, and to protect us from them? Is this "wrapping" not an announcement of their forthcoming resurrection? Indeed, have they not been reabsorbed into foetal life so that they may be born again? When Dietman wraps his thumb or his saw with a plaster, with cotton-wood, with gauze or with cotton, does he do this to "treat" them—does even the most minor utensile deserve our sympathy? Or does he want to symbolize our pathological and irrational relation to our tools?

***

But how can one know for certain that an artist will not, from one moment to the next, return to his previous work-methods and take up his old instruments again? He might be considered a manipulator or an explorer of new sensations; but what must in no way be overlooked is that the artist is essentially governed by tensions and reflections which encourage him to pursue the exploration of his work.

The tendency of the artist to constantly reappraise himself necessarily leads to the reapparaisal of his perception, but he does not apply it to himself (the self-portrait, a great innovation in its time), instead he applies it to the medium of his craft (for example to the frame, which delimited his painting-surface), so that he extends outside of it, renews it, and enters into a space which he had been refused until now.

Painting has entered into a new age, that of second degree art, given that it is self-reflectiveness which is now its ruling principle. It follows that an important trend is visible in today's plastic art, in all its forms, which necessarily leads it to the inclusion of the "third dimension" in order to escape the prevailing optical representation, which is restrictive. Painting's most traditional parameter, namely two-dimensionality, is being called into question. Plasticity turns away from the image to explore the object.

There are thousands of ways for it to reach this point. For instance, instead of merely laying his colours on a canvas, the plastician first rips it up or pierces it. The result is that he thus gives a smooth and homogeneous surface a minimal volume (the width of a piece of cardboard or of material, as a result of tearing it up). Another advantage is that, thanks to the hole which has been opened up this way, it now is possible to reach the other side of the piece of canvas and see what was hidden behind. Apart from tearing it up, one can also crease or layer the canvas; or even crunch up and twist together papers on which one has previously drawn: in this case, as in the others, the artist produces volume. He does not merely stick to "optics," but he invites us to touch his work.

I have examined the unsettling case of the "artists of objectity," who nevertheless have made more efforts to depreciate the object than to praise it, such as Tinguely, who devotes himself entirely to machines which ultimately break down, or—mainly—such as Pop artists, who appear dedicated to manufactured goods when in fact theirs is a mocking and dismissive attitude. Now, in order to strengthen the argument, let us turn to the examination of those who have paved the way for modernity (recognizing objectity and giving a positive evaluation of it).

A few monographic remarks, although limited, are inevitable; moreover, subjective choices have (again) been given a right of place, a fact

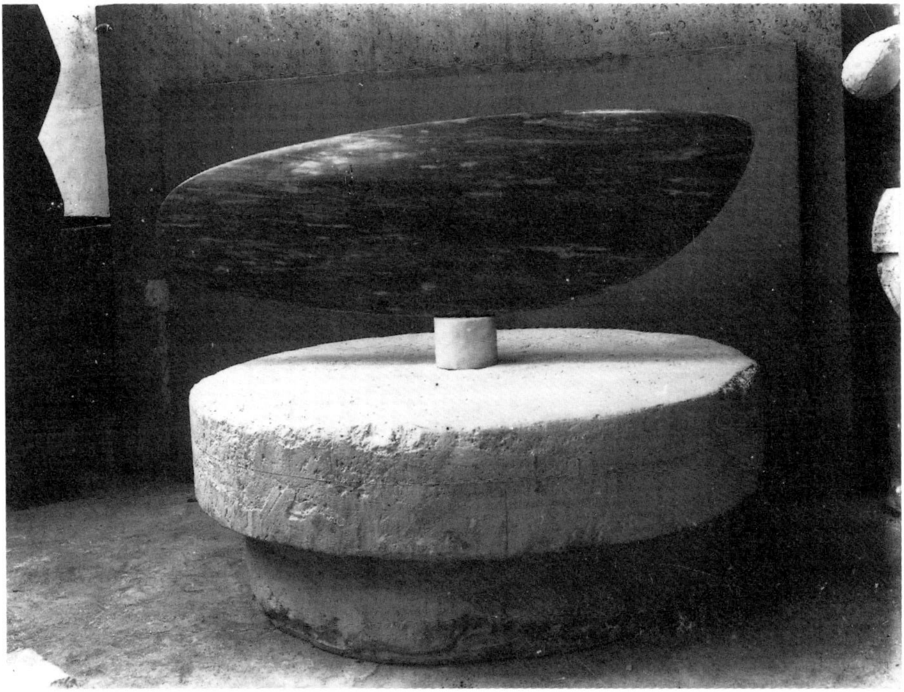

13 – Constantin Brancusi, *Fish*, 1930 (© by ADAGP, Paris 1992)
photo Musée National d'Art Moderne, Paris

which may jeopardize the present thesis.

Let us begin with Zoltan Kemeny (1907-1963) who should certainly provide the best backing for the following comments concerning the evolution of art.

Kemeny's first job was to make shop signs[6] (for innkeepers, cobblers, or pork-butchers of his district); he then studied carpentry, before finally choosing to become a graphic designer and a draughtsman (he even worked for some time as an animator and also as a writer for a Zurich fashion magazine).

On the side, he devoted himself to painting. And in his naive work, inspired by folklore, he soon started to mix solid ingredients in with his colours.

However, he was not to be recognized until the sixties. It was what he called his "relief images" that made him famous. "My number one priority, he declared, is to free my picture from the wall"!

For many reasons, these works are not to be considered sculptures. As will be shown, the boundary between these two branches of constructive art gradually becomes thinner and thinner, and ultimately modern sculpture and painting become one and the same thing.

The basic operation in Kemeny's work is always the same: it consists in assembling thin metal strips, various elements which have been cut up or bent, metallic plates, screws, rivets, bolts—the result is a quivering metal construction! Let us not forget the few pieces of cloth, and little bits of string which he adds to all this, although it is the industrial materials which prevail by far over the rest. The artist proceeds with cutting out, carving and melting the given materials. A blowlamp and a soldering iron are his only tools. Aluminium rods or sheets, or more often strips of cloth and light frameworks are built onto a socle.

As a result, the surface bristles with spikes, it literally "stands on end"; heaps of sheets and rods, of different length and breadth, pointing in different directions, are grouped together.

But why does Kemeny refuse to consider his demiurgic metallic works "sculptures"? Why does he prefer to call them "relief images"?

First, in his opinion, sculpture is still dominated by a latent geometric bias (look at the great number of cubes, columns, pedestals, steles,

(6) — According to biographers and commentators of his work, whom I follow.

and blocks!). It cannot escape the force of gravity, though it plays around with it. Here, things are quite different: the work as a whole produces a whirling effect; sometimes, it consists of nothing more than small particles, nails or ribbons (the construction is light). Besides, Kemeny refers to his executions as "canvases," when he never even uses this means of support. Finally, his works might sometimes be suspended, but they are rarely laid on the ground or put onto a pedestal.

Colour, the artist's favourite "weapon," is a main feature of these metallic half-reliefs—the ochre-like colour of the brass he uses, or the red of copper; as for the aluminium sheet, its colour varies from yellowish to whitish-grey, according to its thickness. In any event, thanks to the rough patches achieved by his implants, he creates an effect of shadow and light. "There is no boundary between the two (painting and sculpture), and my works are painting-sculptures."

Kemeny's pictures do not refer to an external reality (the art based on contemplative vision comes to an end): but does this mean that they are purely arbitrary, imaginary or oniric?

I do not believe this to be the case; besides, the titles of his works give one food for thought: *Visualisation of the Invisible*; *The Connection of Thought with Reality*; *Thought Treated as Form*; *A Cross-Section of Ideological Thought*; *Synthetical Spirit*; *The Skin of an Idea*; *Decyphered Feeling*; *Metallic Mentality*... Thus, *Thought Treated as Form* is a wonderful metallic, whirling "monstration" of the psyche's processes.

This certainly seems to give way to matter which has been endowed with spirit (through a series of connections, windings, irradiations and fittings). Kemeny truly celebrates material substances, be it in sheet, fork, in tree shape, as well as their proliferation. One could mistake his works for beehives, or for things gone mouldy, or even for complex networks of neurons. He confesses to not discriminating between technical and natural elements (although it is obvious that he grants a special status to metallography, neurology, and geomorphology together with the strata he investigates). Interviewed by Michel Ragon in 1959, he declared: "Iron has a heart, nerves. The respiratory system of a plant may be just the same as the molecular system of steel." Indeed, his work as a whole tends towards the depiction of a mixed world, both organic and metallic, a living structure made of alveoli, cells, and corpuscules.

In *Late Night Early Morning*, Kemeny enthusiastically explores a world of contrasts: from the start, iron is used to generate lightness; the most immobile and resistant material appears to flow like a stream (as a result of the way in which the solderer has connected and bent it). So that it evokes dawn as it gradually succeeds to grey night, and as it begins to shed light on a few points of the superimposed blades, the edges of which have been bent down and inwards. On one side of the work is a forest, a dense pile of materials; on its other, light successfully dissipates the remaining darkness thanks to the extremities being bent and to the clustering of elements. *Late Night...* given that the night is on the verge of vanishing: bees are already buzzing among the palm leaves which are still closed. Once again, we are confronted with a bio-mechanical scene, in which the vegetation which has closed at night, is about to open up to daylight.

However, Kemeny claims that he first worked in "two-and-a-half dimensions," that is, not exactly in three, because he wanted to avoid architectural constructions.

Given that classical art has crushed relief, relegating it to the background, and since it prefers to render relief metaphorically instead of effectively, it is time to set it free. Here, then, it stands upright, bristling and buzzing with molecules; it is no longer a representation, but a presentation: this surge upwards and this use of small volumes both reveal a "structure," a complex object (half-way between inert and living matter), which is both apprehensible by sight and touch.

One might object that by singling out Kemeny's work, an individual case has been given too much weight. If others, who have inevitably followed in the same path, have not been mentioned, it is because, in fact, everyone has done so!

Following Kemeny (European), Franck Stella (American) now deserves our attention for many different reasons. He started off with "black paintings," consisting of parallel strips, or of mere lines, at equal intervals (both the most geometric abstraction and the most ascetic minimalism).

Later on, in around 1965, comes the *Protactor* series, which, however, will not be discussed in the present analysis. It nevertheless allows him to make the transition to the present stage. These works mainly consisted of curves and semi-circles stuck against one another, and were above all of gigantic dimensions (several meters), just as though Stella were already attempting to leave the area delimited by the frame, through the sides by means of this lengthhening and stretching process.

In around 1975 however, the artist's evolution necessarily leads him to work with volume, and he sets himself free from representation; hence the assembling of different materials, with garish and glittering colours (using silver, spray-paint—these works appear to be "made-up"). In some cases, it is true, they are not painted in this aggressive way.

Franck Stella teaches us three things:

1) In an interview with Claude Gintz[7], when asked, not very surprisingly, whether these are "painted reliefs or painted constructions," Stella clearly replies: "The only thing that matters to me is that the emphasis should be put on the painting, on the way it is perceived... I mean that in spite of its relief features, the thing you are facing is a painting"; referring to an unpainted Indian bird structure, he also declared: "I would call it a painted relief, which is quite different from a relief sculpture."

2) During a certain period, Stella resorts to a technique—again he assures us it is painting—which proves to be decisive: he uses wire netting and iron frames. How does he go about it? He needs of course to put together everything he has collected (strips, metal pieces which look like blisters, dowels, various kinds of waste), but his aim is to move away from the wall in order to take advantage of the space between it and his materials. Now, thanks to a bent and rounded piece of wire netting, he can hang his more or less multicoloured scraps and cuttings in this very space.

This is an ingenious and cunning device, since it is virtually invisible: the space is thus opened; the traditional frame, which enclosed and imprisoned the work is abandoned, whilst conventional supporting methods (a hindrance and a concealing cover) are also abolished.

This light piping makes possible a montage which turns away, as Stella puts it, from the "representational world," and frees us from two-dimensionality: "One could say that instead of using representational space, I have chosen to use real space. I have done this because I do not

(7) — "Artistes", April 1980, p. 13.

think that there is any choice in the matter.[8]"

3) More surprisingly still, Stella claims that this was a means for him to return to the painting or the art of the Renaissance, in particular to that of Caravaggio.

Artists, at that time, covered both sides of their sheet with drawings, painted both wings of the tryptich, and above all, they made certain to decorate the ceilings and the cupolas of churches and palaces; hence the fresco in relief covering architectural volumes. Painting has exhausted itself in these tasks: its field of application must be widened ("expanded").

Some critics have plainly expressed their reservations concerning these daring constructions (metal pictures glittering with bright reflections); they have applied Baudelaire's comments, which will be discussed later on, to modern art. Since these works have been made clear of the wall (for instance steles, which are really panels joined together, back to back), it is possible for one to walk round them: not only have the various "tricks" used—the stratagem by which the construction was built—become more apparent, but the whole is diluted by the multi-faceted vision, which is quite different altogether from the shock, spark and intensity afforded by the (traditional) frontal approach.

Besides, the constantly re-occurring objection is likely to be raised once more: is this not merely a particular form of art? The answer is that it affected all schools, amongst which two names in particular deserve special mention, since they played an outstanding role in creating this tidal wave.

As early as 1910, Tatlin came up with and exhibited "bas-reliefs," as well as cavo rilievos. In opposition to abstract art, which has too great a tendency to obliterate things, he rehabilitated or even invented the first tectonic constructions. His aim was to place the accent on form, to free it from that which stifled it, and to bring it down from the wall (by producing a hybrid between painting and sculpture). Tatlin's idea of culture and art was that they should be material through and through.

As an artist, he leaned towards the production of prosaic, utensils for everyday use (he had previously designed beds, clothing, crockery, and above all heaters).

Going hand in hand with the above is the shift which has taken place —and which will be subject to further analysis—from the incessant

(8) — Id., p. 7.

grappling of art with volume and with a concrete rendering of reality (an effective rendering of it) to this enormous task of renewing the object, no matter how mean or humble (design).

The fundamental problem of three-dimensionality has also received further attention from Donald Judd: "I have never taken sculpture as a model, although I have been impressed, not exactly influenced, but rather stimulated by a number of people, for instance by Bontecou and by Chamberlain.[9]" Indeed, in referring to Chamberlain's exhibition (emulating César, perhaps?) of compressed, coloured metal sculptures (salvaged from old cars), Judd emphasized the use, and above all the importance of colour, as well as of that of the smooth surfaces reflecting light. He finally decides to make use of the "relief and colour" partnership (the "specific objects"). In his earlier works, he covered his canvases or support materials with a rough, crusty layer of paint, and he even deliberately favoured surfaces including many angular protrusions (similar to the collage, and foreshadowing the process by which the upper layer becomes unstuck from the supporting lower layer). As a logical consequence, he incorporated "real pieces" into these executions. And finally, he started to place his montages in the middle of the exhibition hall: "When I had finished the first two works in the round, I found it surprising having an object standing right in the middle of the room. I found this intriguing. On the one hand, I did not know quite how I felt about it, and on the other, it suddenly seemed to offer a vast number of possibilities.[10]"

Judd added an original touch to his creations by using stainless (and perforated) steel, polished aluminium, galvanized iron, copper, etc. Let us also mention plexiglass, which allows one to see the coloured surfaces on the inside of a given volume; sometimes, Judd also covered the whole thing with lacquer and enamel, in which case, it struck one by its aggressive and overpowering shininess.

Here, chromatic effects prevail over construction; so that, as Judd contends, although pictoriality becomes associated with sculpture, it does not concede any of its rights.

***

(9) — Unpublished transcription of talks held at the Jewish Museum on May 2, 1966.
(10) — *Don Judd : An Interview with John Coplans*, in "Don Judd," Pasadena Art Museum, Exhibition Catalogue, 1971.

Now the reverse question must be considered: does contemporary sculpture not lean towards painting in its turn, as seems most certainly to be the case? If the latter has assimilated three-dimensionality, then it is also true that "spatial art" has assimilated that which has been so carefully developed by pictoriality. Does this imply the merging of the hitherto distinct disciplines?

According to Charles Baudelaire, "sculpture is tiresome" by nature: "[...] it exhibits too many surfaces at once. It is in vain that the sculptor forces himself to take up a unique point of view, for the spectator who moves around the figure can choose a hundred different points of view, except for the right one, and it often happens that a chance trick of the light, an effect of the lamp, may discover a beauty which is not at all the one the artist had in mind—and this is a humiliating thing for him. A picture, however, is only what it means to be; there is no other way of looking at it than on its own terms.[11]"

True, Baudelaire was too quick to close the door by which sculpture subsequently escaped from its apparent constitutional inferiority: he rejects any possible mixture between art forms. "What healthy brain could imagine without horror a painting in relief, a piece of sculpture mechanically activated, a rhymeless ode, a novel in verse, and so on? When the natural aim of an art is misunderstood, it is natural to call to its aid all the devices which are alien to that art.[12]" Baudelaire thundered forth against a sculptor who exhibited "a lilliputian world" at the Salon: "This lilliputian world, these miniature processions, these little crowds which wind in and out among the rocky boulders, put one simultaneously in mind of the relief maps in the Marine Museum, of musical picture-clocks, and of those landscapes with fortress, drawbridge and the changing of the guard which may be seen in pastry-cooks' and toy-sellers' shops.[13]"

It is not difficult to imagine how irritated he may have felt in the presence of "the Caribs of the wrinkle, the hair and the wart (like M. David).[14]"

The poet of "modernity" finally opts for an academic form of art

(11) — Baudelaire, "Why sculpture is tiresome," *The Salon of 1846*, in *Art in Paris 1845-1862. Salons and other Exhibitions reviewed by Charles Baudelaire*, translated and edited by Jonathan Mayne, Phaidon Press, London, 1965, p.111.

(12) — Baudelaire, "Sculpture," *The Salon of 1859*, in *Art in Paris*, p. 208.

(13) — Baudelaire, *The Salon of 1859*, p. 208.

(14) — Baudelaire, "Why sculpture is tiresome," *The Salon of 1846*, p. 112.

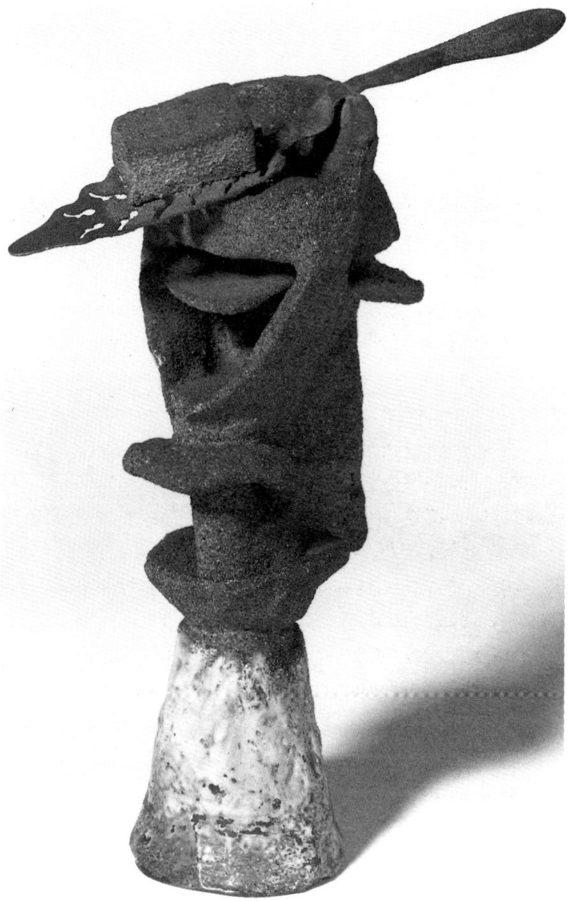

14 – Picasso, *the Glass of Absinth*, 1914 (© by SPADEM, Paris 1992)
photo Musée National d'Art Moderne, Paris

which maintains the old divisions. He underrates any type of exchange: first, modern sculpture has renounced hard materials, namely stone, marble, iron, or even wood, and instead, it frequently uses soft ones, for instance plaster, clay, all that can be melted and fused, plastics of all sorts; it has a tendency to reject monumentalism, as well as theatricality, as illustrated by Maillol's, Bourdelle's, even Pompon's works, which continue to be burdened by overabundance, by ornamental and picturesque elements. It prefers lightness, openwork, empty spaces: it substitutes the interplay of lines and planes for massive and compact constructions.

One could also bring in the Futurist Boccioni, who openly fuses the two arts (*Technical Manifesto of Futurist Painting*), by extricating them from the impasse in which they are both trapped. Both sculpture and painting are guilty of depicting things as separate and isolated, as a result of the prevalence given to an optical approach which renders things immobile. The distances separating objects need to be abolished: divisions and clear-cut outlines are most artificial devices. "Our bodies enter into the sofas on which we sit, and the sofas enter into us, as also the tram that runs between the houses enters into them, and they in turn hurl themselves onto it and fuse with it.[15]"

Most importantly, Boccioni stated a basic principle of composition. Just as the Impressionists relied on the juxtaposition of complementary colours to bring out their vibrant and intense quality, the plastician, be he a sculptor or a painter, must make use of complementary forms which will ensure that the composition, besides its special chromatic qualities, also has a special dynamic quality. Boccioni advocates the opposition and simultaneously the combination of contrasting shapes, the interpenetration, if possible, of contrasting planes and volumes.

However, Alexander Archipenko (1887-1964), a militant for painting-sculpture, was even more forceful in the advice he gave, and should contribute to strengthening my argument.

As Apollinaire wrote in 1912, "his art is moving closer and closer to absolute sculpture, and one day it should merge with absolute painting and absolute architecture, thus giving rise once more to pure plasticity,

(15) — Boccioni, *Technical Manifesto of Futurist Painting*, quoted in *Concepts of Modern Art*, edited by Nikos Stangos, Thames and Hudson, London, reprinted 1990, p. 99 (Translators' note).

reaching beyond any style, any technique, any methods."

It would be very difficult to find another specialist in the art of carving and constructing who fought the visual world with such obstinacy: "painting-sculptures" was the term he used to refer to his works.

He turned to the empty space as a solution, which counterbalances, and above all restricts the solid parts. In this way, he placed the accent on concavity, although he avoided doing so systematically: "the materiality of the non-being is a fundamental concept of sculpture. But drilling holes in a statue, or purposelessly carving out cavities is absurd if it is done systematically, without any real symbolic motives."

Besides, Archipenko produced a large number of luminous, and even of polychromatic sculptures (*Manifesto of Polychromy*). To that end, he used plexiglass or aluminium sheets, both of which have the property of enhancing the transparency of a mass. Besides, he would add a hidden source of light in order to increase the luminousness of the sculpture.

"What is the cause of the decline of polychromatic sculpture? Is it the result of the irrational theory which has it that pure form can only be found in monochromatic matter? Do we not admire the multicoloured shapes of birds, flowers, etc.?[16]"

Different neologisms have been coined, among which "sculptecture," combining sculpture, painting, and architecture. It is only right that it should be applied to this pioneer, to this passionate investigator of the relation between volume and colour. As early as 1924, he invented an ingenious device which he called the "Archipentura"; it consisted in a series of metal strips (a hundred and ten of them) which he placed horizontally, one on the top of the other. Thanks to a mechanism inserted in the frame, the strips change position so that the picture gradually changes. This movement—one work enclosing several ones—implies that a step into the real space has been made, and it also means the end of immobility as well as of two-dimensionality.

Thus, it appears that if sculpture is headed towards painting, painting in turn is moving closer to sculpture, so that the final result is their fusion.

Once again, I hear the same old objections: namely that these achievements are mere circus acts, tricks, quite irrelevant to either modern or other forms of real art, which feed on sufferings, passions, and spiritual

(16) — Archipenko, "Manifeste de la polychromie", in *Oeuvres, Visionnaire international*, 1969, p. 23.

revolutions. How dare one reduce it to such artful tricks? Art must not be turned into a sort of "techno-poetics." Shame on the contemporary artist, who relies too heavily on recipes!

Are critics not guilty here of mystification? Valéry declared war on the old myths of creation, and on the clichés concerning inspiration. Thanks to him, "doing" enters victoriously into the arena of artistic work, and is even recognized as its constitutive feature. Let us renounce, once and for all, the notion of a "being" which it is the artist's task to gradually uncover, and which he approaches with great trembling!

Furthermore, modern art, having gone full circle, meets up again with tradition (think for instance of polychromatic statues). To disapprove of it is to condemn the ancients, who are still greatly considered and admired.

So that he who discovers a new material approach, or even just a new technique, of which he explores the possibilities, fully deserves a better standing and our praise. Another great accomplishment is the discovery of hitherto unknown provinces of the universe, or else the use of a tool which has never been handled before—or better still, the use of either ignored or totally new materials.

That is why the sculptors of non-materiality—such as Boccioni and Archipenko—have deserved so much attention: they originate an irresistible trend. Let us add Brancusi to the list, who brings confirmation, if such confirmation is at all possible, that "sculpture-painting" is the present trend in plasiticity—its royal road, even—(the "images in relief" before the installation itself, which is more three-dimensional than ever, in the middle of the exhibition hall). Soon, movement is added to and assimilated by volume, which is made to include "time," "change," and, as a result, four-dimensionality.

No one challenged gravity as resolutely as Brancusi, who resorted to slenderness and to the utmost lack of ornementation (his bird, his fish). This new form of sculpture lets loose a "minimalist" fury. "Straighforward carving," says Brancusi, "is the real path towards sculpture, but it also is the worst one for those who have not learned to walk."

Here, there is no pomposity, no bombast (as opposed to "steak-sculpture," as Brancusi puts it to emphasize its tendency to pump up the muscles of athletes). Brancusi achieves a clear and smooth volume.

Let us take a close look at his fish (see fig. 13). No fin, no scales, no tail, no head: it is reduced to the mere property of aquatic dynamism, to an ellipse, to a pure shape devoid of any accidents.

Brancusi's main purpose was the concentration of light and its reflection. His sculpture no longer sought to arrive at a closed volume (the cube, the parallelepiped, the block), but the aim was, instead, to outline and to hollow out as much as possible in order to obtain a surface or a mirror. Fluidity and slimness prevail. "My whole life has been spent exploring flight," flight in the case of birds, and, in the case of fish, its equivalent, swimming.

The example of the fish demonstrates that Brancusi fully exploited the dark veins of marble, the brightness of certain milky stones, the golden hue of bronze, the blue shade of certain rocks. In every one of his works, the emphasis was placed on reflection and light, which were captured with the help of mirror-like surfaces.

Elementary shapes triumph over more complex ones: the ellipse rather than the circle, the cone or the pyramid rather than the cube, the solomonic column rather than the shaft.

With its tendency to reduce, to outline, to make slender, and with the use of colours, the main features of sculpture have evidently been abandoned (suppleness and flexibility have been given priority). Hence the reunification, under our very eyes, of the two arts—painting and sculpture—which have been contrasted for so long. If one is to achieve multi-dimensional plasticity, the fusion of the two is necessary in the process of the construction. (As Kemeny put it a long time ago, even if painting were detached from the rest, it would still be in "two-and-a-half dimensions" given its leaning towards the ronde-bosse or the bas relief).

The object must be to fill an isotropic space, to "resuscitate" it, to force it out of its homogeneity and help it recover from its exhaustion. It has been undervalued for too long, whereas too much work has been done on the flat surface. Let us open it up! For art aspires to plenitude.

***

Those who are most reluctant to accept the conclusions which are presently being drawn would argue that if it is at all legitimate to speak of a "liberation" from the "yoke" of representation, it is only so for a short moment in time, and for a certain school.

They would ask: why attribute absolute value to this notion of "liberation"? Why attempt to place it at the summit of a so-called evolutionary curve? Why consider it the essence of sculpture-painting, that which has triumphed over its former limits? Is this not to forget that by imposing restrictions on expression, one arrives at better results (with "almost nothing" in terms of means, the best, in other words the most condensed form, is achieved)?

The first stage of my answer would be that artists of all leanings have yielded to this liberating force: it can neither be considered a passing phase, nor merely circumstantial. The days of the flat surface are gone for ever. Even in those cases, where the plastician has returned to two-dimensionality, after having gone through the obligatory phase of experimentation with volume, the former gains in relief and size, so that it is renewed.

A brilliant example of the liberation from the picture is Picasso, who was in turn Fauvist, Cubist, and Surrealist (and even, at times, a talented painter of classical pastiches). Cubism was particularly conducive to this, as has already been shown: illusory representation of things depicted from a single perspective was replaced by the brutal vision of things portrayed from many different angles simultaneously (giving rise to virtual volume, to a war on appearance and on the consecutive location of things in space).

Does Collage not also contain in embryo the will to go beyond restrictions and the aspiration, albeit a timid one, to three-dimensionality?

This strategy has often given way to a misunderstanding which must be cleared up: Aragon warned us against confusing two quite separate operations, which one tends to combine: on the one hand, the artist replaces that which he wants to paint (a page from a newspaper or the canework of a chair) by the thing itself, as if merely to avoid unnecessary work. Instead of an image, he presents us with reality. On the other hand, and completely different from the first type of operation, the artist includes in his deceptive painting a piece of real life (a tube ticket, a lock of hair, a string or a piece of material), unrelated to the theme, but which is meant to give weight to that which is being painted, as if a little matter could cancel an optical illusion. The weight of the signifier thus supposedly compensates for the futility of the signified or of appearance. Picasso makes use of both types of collage, no doubt, starting off with the first type, most probably, and then going on to create the second. So that the revolutionary act is governed and can be explained in terms of evolution.

The Glass of Absinth (1914) or *The Guitar* (1926) are examples of Picasso's unequalled devotion to the cause of radical art.

The guitar is really only a piece of pierced sacking: it includes nails, with their pointed ends sticking out (signifying the work's tendency to turn away from the wall, to liberate itself from all forms of ties and to project itself into the open space). It also includes bits of newspapers and two real strings.

More and more, Picasso applied himself to creating painted sculptures and ceramics which he decorated, as well as montages using tubes; like so many others, he also used scraps for his relief-pictures.

"I even heard him complain once," said Aragon, "because all those who came to see him and saw him give life to old pieces of tulle or cardboard, to bits of string or corrugated iron, to material found in dustbins, thought they were doing him a favour by bringing him cuttings of rich fabrics to use in his paintings. He would have none of this: what he wanted was real waste produced by human life, all that was poor, dirty and despised.[17]"

This is not to say that he took delight in repulsive or vile things, but that he turned for help to these pieces of reality, because they contained greater significance and weight than new things. Their value lies not only in their very fragmentariness, but also in the many vicissitudes through which they have passed (mackled or crushed paper, rusty iron, torn material). They bear the marks of handling and usage within their wounded and frayed frame.

Even during the period in which he devoted himself uniquely to pictoriality, Picasso mixed in sand and sawdust with his colours in order to give them a granite-like texture, to confer the beginnings of relief upon them: he saves them in this way from their brilliance and their play with light (decorative and smooth painting). The way was thus paved for the brutal revolt which followed. The importance of his repeated rejection of the flat surface in favour of a wider space, in which all sorts of metamorphoses were operated, must not be underestimated. He created, for instance, a bull's head out of a bicycle handlebar and saddle; he also

(17) — Aragon, *les Collages*, "La peinture au défi," Hermann, Paris, 1980, p. 70

transformed a vase into the figure of a woman, whose hands are hidden behind her back, and whose elongated body is streaked with wavy, oceanic stripes, like Aphrodite or Venus emerging from the waters. He also designed an aerial structure (*Construction*, 1930).

This fanatical iconoclast even managed to build a structure out of filiform shafts, where the empty spaces outweigh the solid ones. In short, then, it cannot be overlooked that throughout his career as a painter, Picasso was constantly attracted to sculptural techniques, and the surge of bizarre assemblages bears witness to this.

Picasso is only one example amongst many. For no artist resisted the temptation of widening the field of art, of totalizing it. The surface had received too much attention. It was necessary to find a way of overcoming saturation, a way out. Collage was first to take a step in the direction of "anti-representation." Consequently, art rushed out into the open space created by the open door. Representation has been abandoned, and instead, art now confronts us with materials, both new and old—for those which have come down to us from the past have not yet exhausted their ability to enchant us (wood can still be burnt, charred, floated, dried, not to mention the various ways in which its knots, its texture or its fissuring may be displayed). A piece of stone or metal can, in turn, be sawn, broken, cut up, worn or sliced. It can be tied to a similar piece of stone or metal (by a given joint, which can either be supple or rigid). The possibilities are endless: it is not in the least surprising that they have given rise to such a passion for assemblage.

The objection which has been made repeatedly is renewed with still greater violence: it is meaningless in art to talk of direction, evolution or progress, as is the case in the present argument.

Now, Harold Rosenberg has severely condemned the likes of Judd or Stella, accusing them of the worst sins: academism, dogmatism, terrorism, and avant-gardist chauvinism!

The anti-art of which they stand accused is supposedly detectable in the will to bring into the work of art unrefined nature, as if unadulterated and unprocessed reality were superior to the rest. However, when condemning something, one necessarily caricatures it. Does Collage deserve to be blamed too? The answer is no! And if it is not the case, it is because double standards are at work! So that if "progress" is incompatible with art as it

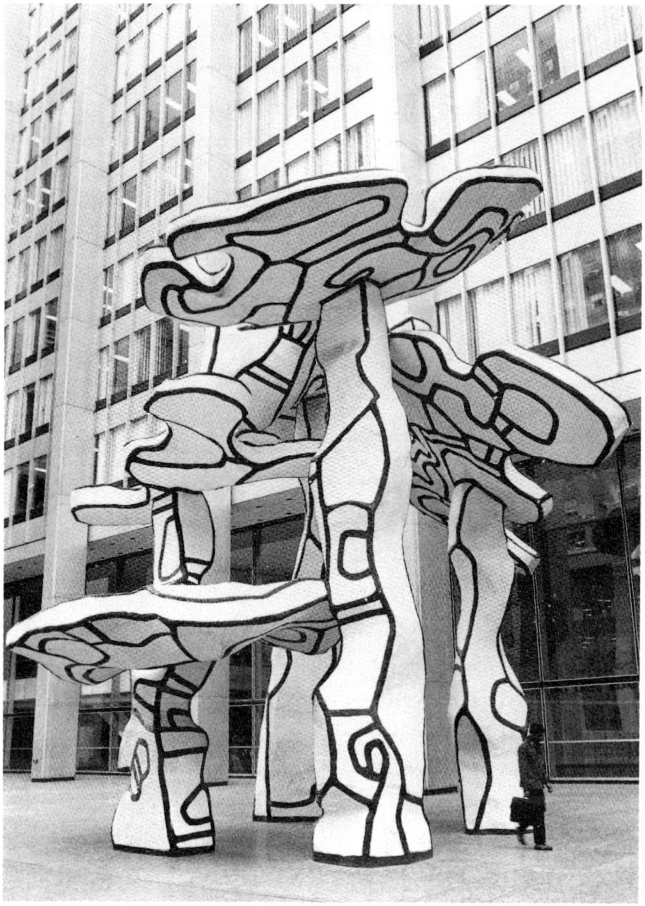

15 – Dubuffet, *Four Trees*, 1972 (© by ADAGP, Paris 1992)
photo Fondation Dubuffet

certainly is, perpetual change, on the contrary, is one of its necessary requirements.

To return to traditional representation would be totally absurd. One is free to maintain this old point of view, but it is advisable to revise it. And this is precisely what becomes increasingly difficult.

In order to clinch the argument, let us now turn to Dubuffet, an exceptional artist, whose importance stems from his ability to vary and renew his practices. His constant shifts are the sign of an insatiable taste for materiality. He does not restrict himself to the surface and turns away from "epidermal" drawings and outlines.

Of the many stumbling blocks facing the plastician, two should be mentioned here: first, the page, the pencil, the sheet of paper, the ink pen, the paint brush and any instrument which requires one to remain on the surface. Secondly, the rigidity of traditional sculpting materials, such as marble and bronze, which have something "funerary" about them.

Plastic materials, and especially polystyrene (light, snowy, proliferating, easy to divide and to fuse again, convenient to paint) made it possible for Dubuffet to create his "Hourloupe cycle" and to develop his "hourloupean structures" (the artist coined this term, which evokes the swell of the sea ("houle"), a scream ("hurlement"), even a mean trick ("entourloupe")—in other words a jumble of resonances, a profusion of ideas, and confusion as to localization).

In classical art, according to Dubuffet, to draw was to look out from a skylight, a window from which to look out onto the world: the artist, though, finally became trapped in this kind of perspective. Dubuffet aimed, on the contrary, to replace representation with the very "presentation" of reality. He preferred things to remain indistinct[18]: his sculpture favoured mixture, hotchpotch and meandering matter (his art of volume owes its existence to resine and to polyester). On assemblage, he wrote: "I have had much recourse to it in my work. I believe the principle of juxtaposing disparate pieces to be most fruitful in the creative process [...] In order for thought to be able to spread its wings and to take off, it needs to be confronted with many different things simultaneously. Many different

(18) — For greater detail, the reader may want to refer to other texts I have written on the subject: "Rematérialiser" (the pages devoted to Jean Dubuffet) and "la Pensée de l'impensable" (introduction to the catalogue of the Galerie Nationale du Jeu de Paume), *Jean Dubuffet, les dernières années*, Paris, 1991.

perspectives, many different aims, even if these contradict each other.[19]"

And again: "If one is forced to use the terminology according to which to draw well is to reproduce things exactly as one sees them, then I would argue that art begins when one learns to draw badly; the worse the drawing, the more creative it is.[20]" These must not be seen as mere jests, witticisms or provocation! Why not take them seriously, since they come from one who has dazzled us with his weightless volumes and with his environmental art (even Land Art has not achieved more than he has in this field)?

And the results are:

a) Multi-faceted monuments of gigantic proportions, such as the four twelve-meter high trees which are bound together. They constitute an exceptional illustration for the present case—and there are many more like them.

b) An amazing series of bottles, coffeemakers, jugs, telephones, all connected up with each other in sinuous networks.

c) Finally, "expanded" paintings (so called because they are made from expanded plastic, into which air is blown), and painted sculptures. Dubuffet devotes himself to showing up matter in all its forms: he catches it in the act of swelling (as with mixed pastes), of leaking (when matter runs or rises), or of fissuring.

No more need be said. Dubuffet celebrates with unequalled zest and vitality art's emancipation from the surface and its rejection of the old rules.

(19) — Jean Dubuffet, *Bâtons rompus*, Editions de Minuit, Paris, 1986, p. 16-17.
(20) — Id., p. 23.

CHAPTER IV

The object's move towards art

If contemporary art tends towards monumental achievements in some cases, and towards effective achievements in all cases (concrete art)—towards that which has been referred to as the aesthetics of montage and of installation-works throughout the discussion—the reverse is also true, though on a smaller scale: the access of furniture, chairs, lighting, typewriters, kettles and utensils generally, to an art which renews them and which reconciles creation with the manufacturing processes of the factory.

Fernand Léger, who was certain that this endeavour would meet with success, said: "The beautiful is everywhere, in the arrangement of a set of saucepans, in a white kitchen wall as well as in a museum.[1]"

But can this possibly be true? Is he not playing a joke on us? Is art really compatible with the reality of daily life, with the fork, the watch or with the frames of a pair of glasses? If so, is this not the sign of decline?

The credibility of the present thesis depends on the distinction, amongst the jumble of prosaic objects, between those which are strictly utilitarian on the one hand (the toothbrush, the mustard pot, the lemon-squeezer, even though Philippe Starck, whose work will be discussed later, worked with these objects)[2], and on the other hand, those objects which are certainly utilitarian, but which contain in addition a cultural dimension (the bottle, the seat, the sideboard or the cupboard).

Admittedly, the dividing-line is shaky: for instance, electric pylons, turbines, and even whole factories have been left to industrial architects, who have sought to create a harmony between these kinds of constructions and their environment, when hitherto only productivity has been taken

(1) — Fernand Léger, *Functions of Painting*, The Viking Press, New York, 1973, p. 63-64.
(2) — In fact, the toothbrush and the kettle had already been taken into consideration by Denis Santachiara.

into account (cathedrals of the modern world). They might not make them "beautiful," but they have succeeded in saving them from what was as a rule ugliness.

Indeed, the art of design raises the status of even the humblest of objects. When it cannot transform them (as in the case of the totally functional object, constituted of scrap iron, dirty oil and filth), it turns to the device of wrapping or streamlining (the art of coachbuilding, or of constant repackaging). The metallic inside is concealed thanks to an attractive exterior envelope, generally smooth and bright; at the same time, this packaging protects both the motor from external (atmospheric) factors and the person who operates it.

In order to overcome the difficulties created by goods which refuse to be put in either category, one must distinguish between the design of the components themselves, which impinges on the object, and a more cosmetic design, that of the façade, which is aimed at that which surrounds the object.

The word "design"—both an English and a French term—has at least two meanings: that of a programme, or of a plan, implying a project, and that of drawing; indeed, the plastician's first task is to put down his conception of the object on paper (only afterwards is the mould made which will enable production on a large scale, standardization and multiplication).

In the past, the aim of the craftsman (the potter, for instance) was to gradually give shape to an original form. Now, however, execution (after having relegated the resulting form to the background) is in turn being relegated by a still more important operation: the establishing of a "set of possibilities," the setting up of a project, the conceptual design of the object.

***

The nature of this art, the question of whether it is art at all, its result and its criterion all raise difficulties and call it into question.

A variety of levels are discernable in even the most trivial of objects; the three most obvious ones are the utilitarian level (the use one makes of it), the ergonomical level (the facilitation of handling) and the commercial level (the goal being to flatter the potential buyer). Now, these morphogenetic requirements stifle symbolism: so, how may one reconcile utility with art, these two enemy forces?

One needs only take a look at a Zulu spoon (from South Africa) exhibited in 1991 at the Dapper Museum amongst a hundred other such spoons: anthropomorphic in inspiration, it is made up of a pair of outstretched legs, a head and two breasts; it was used in the offering of food to masks, in religious ceremonies or in the preparation of special feasts. It "de-profaned" the food it touched, stirred or offered. For us today, its attraction lies in its strangeness, its elongation, in the light weight of the wood from which it is sculpted and in its meaning (a human body is used to feed man—there is more to the object than its blind automatic functional purpose). And yet it is precisely its maladjustement as a utensil which is its main shortcoming.[3]

The usual tendency has been renewed here: form, which generally absorbs or determines function, to the point of cancelling any other consideration, is disconnected from function.

There is a simplistic and damaging theory that attempts to bring the two together: "form follows function" (see Sullivan), whereby the latter has priority over and dictates the former. But an object may have many, sometimes contradictory functions. Which one should be highlighted? An object is "functional" if it takes up only a small amount of space and can be easily fitted away (folding chairs, glasses, and even spoons which are put away in compartmented baskets). But an object is also considered functional if it is easy to maintain or to repair, if, for instance, it is easy to re-solder: so that in this case, the criterion is its modifiability or its removability, etc.

What is more, that which was once considered functional can become a liability and be rejected: take for example the wooden piece of furniture, the marquetry of which starts to spring due to the central heating and dehydrating atmosphere of our modern housing. The set of drawers starts to crack, the chair to crumble and the sofa to flake off! It becomes neces-

(3)—In his book "Afrique noire: la création plastique" (*l'Univers des Formes—Hors de l'Histoire*, Gallimard, 1962), Michel Leiris reproduces an incredible variety of these kitchen tools which despite their modest constitution (a simple handle and a hollow oval part at its end) rival with the human body: the handling of food which they enable (thanks to their adjustment to the mouth) is in itself of great importance. Nonetheless, its function is of little importance in comparison with the meaning and the gravity of the operation.

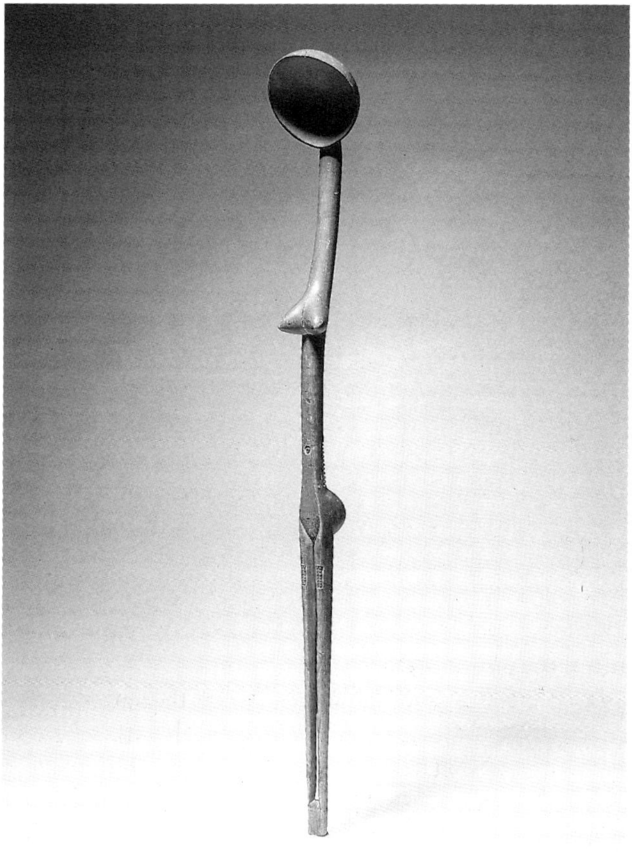

16 – Zulu Spoon – South Africa. (© coll. Musée de l'Homme, Paris)
photo Destable Lemzadoua

sary, therefore, for the sake of solidity—a new requirement, to which the product must now live up—to have recourse to materials which are more resistant than they were and which are able to sustain a new environment.

Besides, the famous, though vain and empty formula "form follows function" has given way to a reply now widespread: "form follows fiasco"!

In short, Sullivan's thesis is not valid: first, because of the many different roles the object takes on (how to determine which one has the upper hand?), and secondly—and above all—because it is wrong that the most essential aspect (the aesthetic dimension) should be sacrificed and erased by the mere instrumental function: by doing so, one does not solve the dilemma, one suppresses it instead.

The problem is the following: how may one combine the two extremes without slipping into mannerist extravagance and into gratuitous decoration on the one hand; and on the other, how may one ensure that the duality or juxtaposition of the two does not undermine the unity which is being sought? How, within the very frame of the object, may one overcome the antinomy between its positive being—its real function or its content—and its appearance, which must be suitable, but to which it must not be reduced?

The domestic object is in need of renovation and even of creation, but it is far from having overcome all the obstacles. It confronts us with a real methodological riddle: how to conceive the object and do justice at the same time to all its components?

The history of the endeavours made to save the object does not go back very far, but, paradoxically, that which was supposed to free it contributed to crushing and demolishing it with even greater force than before!

At first, war was declared on machinery and on routine production which had pushed the craftsman and the creator aside. What is more, the factory, accused of spreading "ugliness" everywhere, covered its products with superfluous elements, leading to the undesirable separation between the object itself and the sophisticated ornamentation, beneath which it hid (rococo flourishes).

Art Nouveau, which is still in France derisively called "Modern Style" in protest (an example of French anglophobia!), or "Tiffany Style," after one of its principal figures, who worked in the United States, and sometimes even more caustically "style nouille" ("Spaghetti Style"), owed its existence to a revolt, seeking to free dishes, the stove, the ash-tray, the vase or the lighter from their cheap-looking aspect due to uniform standardization.

Consequently, it either celebrated the return to a glorious past—*the gothic revival*—preferably a medieval past with its drawbridges, its turrets and its crenels, or else, it looked to nature for inspiration: bibelots were covered with floral motifs. Ruskin and his disciple, Morris, popularized this crusade, or rather this agitation: wallpapers and vases alike were decorated with arabesques and sinuous lines.

Is this perhaps one of the first manifestations of design? Art Nouveau certainly has a few comparable features, such as the desire to save the ordinary object from mere utilitarianism and from mediocrity, as well as to save it from its ontological insignificance and to see in it an emblem (a "medium" onto which things can be added). But why conceal the object under so many garlands and so much fruit? Instead of elevating it, one is disguising it in flashy rags. Indeed, the movement soon spends its force, due to the excesses it commits in decoration, but also due to the fact that it is from resentment, from an opposition to the machine that it draws its inspiration.

Admittedly, the French School of Nancy (the ceramist and glass artist, Émile Gallé, and the cabinet-maker Majorelle) produced pyrotechnics: it is to them we owe the creation of dishes with inlaid peonies and irises, and of glasses with dragonflies—besides, there is an inscription by Gallé which reads: "the vase is a fruit." Their easily identifiable furniture and twisted ironwork representing branches and flowers are just as unforgettable.

Molten glass allowed for all sorts of exhilarating possibilities when experimenting with form and polychromy: sheets of varying transparency were superimposed and powder inserted between them. Their vitrification produced new and subtle effects and trailing infiltrations, resulting in unique opalescent, shimmering effects and colour gradations. The success of the School of Nancy also lies in the fact that it does not concern itself with objects which are too prosaic, concentrating mainly on vases, goblets and lamps—in other words, objects which are not linked to basic needs and bodily functions (feeding, cooking, hygiene), such as the kettle, the frying pan or the toothbrush, to which the modern designer subsequently turns.

Art Déco—which was the main trend during the 1925 Decorative Arts exhibition, hence its name—reacted predictably by abolishing excessively sinuous lines ("le coup de fouet," literally "a whip lash"), and all fussiness. Instead, it aspired to simplicity, to order and to austerity, without renouncing, however, the former naturalist credo (the basket of fruit and the garland of flowers). This art form no longer stood in opposition to the mechanical model: it sometimes brought aeroplane-wings, portholes and cogwheels into its style. Neither did it continue to reject modern materials—bakelite, beaten copper, chromium-plated steel —, on the contrary, whereas "Modern Style" had refused to use these and has turned principally to wood or stone. Leaves, insects and palm-trees continued to appear, but in a less contorted and precious manner: everything was stylized. As for Art Déco's fruit and flowers, these were diagrammatic, in vaguely cubist fashion.

Bauhaus, which spread its influence throughout Europe, imposed a much more radical vision of things, venerating geometric functionalism and rejecting decoration as a whole ("the ornament is criminal"). Cuttlery, ventilators and door knobs were transformed, frills and rocaille had vanished! Instead, there were metallic tubular chairs and prefabricated boxes for housing. Whenever it was possible to do so, simple elements were combined: it seems that their respective position in relation to each other had become the new criterion, replacing the heavy substantiality of furniture and household appliances.

The Bauhaus example is an illustration of the difficulty of arriving at a stable conception of the object: it wavers between a theatrical approach to the object, and one of ultra-simplification, reducing the object to its bare bones!

By attempting to reduce the object at all costs, the Bauhaus movement leads to its impoverishment. It tries so hard to rid it of ornementation that it undermines it at the same time: the result of doing away with "appearance," considered elitist and arbitrary, is that finally, there remains nothing at all.

So that it was only natural for Bauhaus to be swept away in its turn.

Besides, it contained inherent contradictions which precipitated its fall.

A good example is Le Corbusier, a fervent follower of the group and a close friend of Gropius. He was the greatest expounder of the need for an economy of means and was a firm believer in the aesthetic superiority of pure form, stripped of its deceptive layer and its fake abundance. One only need read his *Defense of Enamel Paint*, or his treatise on *Lime Water*: "It is every citizen's duty to replace his wall coverings, his damask, his wallpapers, his stencils with a simple layer of white enamel paint.[4]"

This iconoclast, declaring war on all forms of decoration, joins the Bauhaus in its intransigent asceticism. It is possible to see in this a return, *mutatis mutandis*, to the century-old conflict between the (northern) Reformation, hostile to images, and the (southern) Counter-Reformation, which celebrates them on the contrary, and progressively gives in to facile methods prescribed by blind superstition. The two sides are involved in an aesthetic conflict: on the one hand, total bareness, and on the other, overwhelming plasiticity. Le Corbusier's attitude was the same towards towns and housing: he felt that their convolutedness threatened to crush and to asphyxiate us, that overcrowding would lead to congestion.

Following Bauhaus example, Le Corbusier makes valuable analyses in favour of new materials which lead to revolutionary methods (streamlined iron, reinforced concrete, water-proof coatings, clinker). These alone—hence the importance of constitutive materials for the proper distinction and understanding of the object—have the obligation and the ability to renew the framework of both housing and objects: "A house is a living-machine. Baths, sun, hot and cold water, the desired temperature, preservation of food, hygiene, beauty resulting from proportions. An armchair is a sitting-machine, etc.: Maple showed the way. A ewer is a washing-machine: Twyford created these. Our modern lifestyle, our activity in general—except for those moments when we sit down to an old-fashioned tea—has led to the creation of these objects: modern suits, pens, eversharps, typewriters, telephones, beautiful desks [...] Gillette

(4) — Le Corbusier, *l'Art décoratif aujourd'hui*, Arthaud, "l'Esprit nouveau," 1981, p. 191. He is full of praise for the "nothing," which abolishes the medley of colours and intrusive decoration, and he recommends bareness. "It is the hollow of Narcissus' hand which led to the invention of the bottle; Diogenes' barrel, already quite an improvement on our protective organs, [...] is the basic cell of the house...".

razors and English pipes, bowler hats and limousines, liners and aeroplanes.[5]"

The reason for stressing this is that Le Corbusier himself attributed great importance to methods of construction. For it is these methods, for instance, which may cause the object to change its usual shape and take on perhaps unlimited proportions. The object is transfigured to the extent that it is no longer possible to maintain its previous status (namely an anthropomorphic appearance).

Thus, "[...] for a ground floor of a fifty-storey building, the use of thick walls which were once a necessity has persisted, whereas thin glass or brick partitions would do the job just as well.

In a city like Prague, for example, there is an outdated regulation whereby the walls of the top room of the house must be forty-five centimeters thick, and that at each floor down, an additional fifteen centimeters must be added, which means that the walls of some buildings can attain a width of one meter and fifty centimeters by the time they reach the ground floor. Today, the use of big blocks of soft stones leads to the paradox that windows, designed to get light, are reduced to deep embrasures, undermining the initial intention.[6]"

In short, Le Corbusier's aim is to let air into the dying cities. The town planning he advocates is one where towers are surgically "implanted" and where the ground is freed and filled with greenery. In the same vein, he propounds light and sober house-interiors.

There would be no subject of complaint were it not for the fact that this spokesman for machines, for modernism, for new materials and for simple forms, flies into the arms of his enemy, Ruskin himself, in that his indictment soon takes the shape of the glorification of sovereign nature.

Le Corbusier's reason for this is undoubtedly to make his utopian geometrism more acceptable *in extremis*, but it only contributes to making the project as a whole ambiguous, and even self-contradictory.

Besides, the machine which cuts, polishes and produces is only given pride of place because it outdoes nature: the latter is deemed to function irregularly, and this needs to be corrected.

The spider's web and Diogenes' barrel are perfect epitomizations.

(5) — Le Corbusier, *Vers une architecture*, G. Crès et Cie, Paris, pp. 71, 73.
(6) — Id., p. 71.

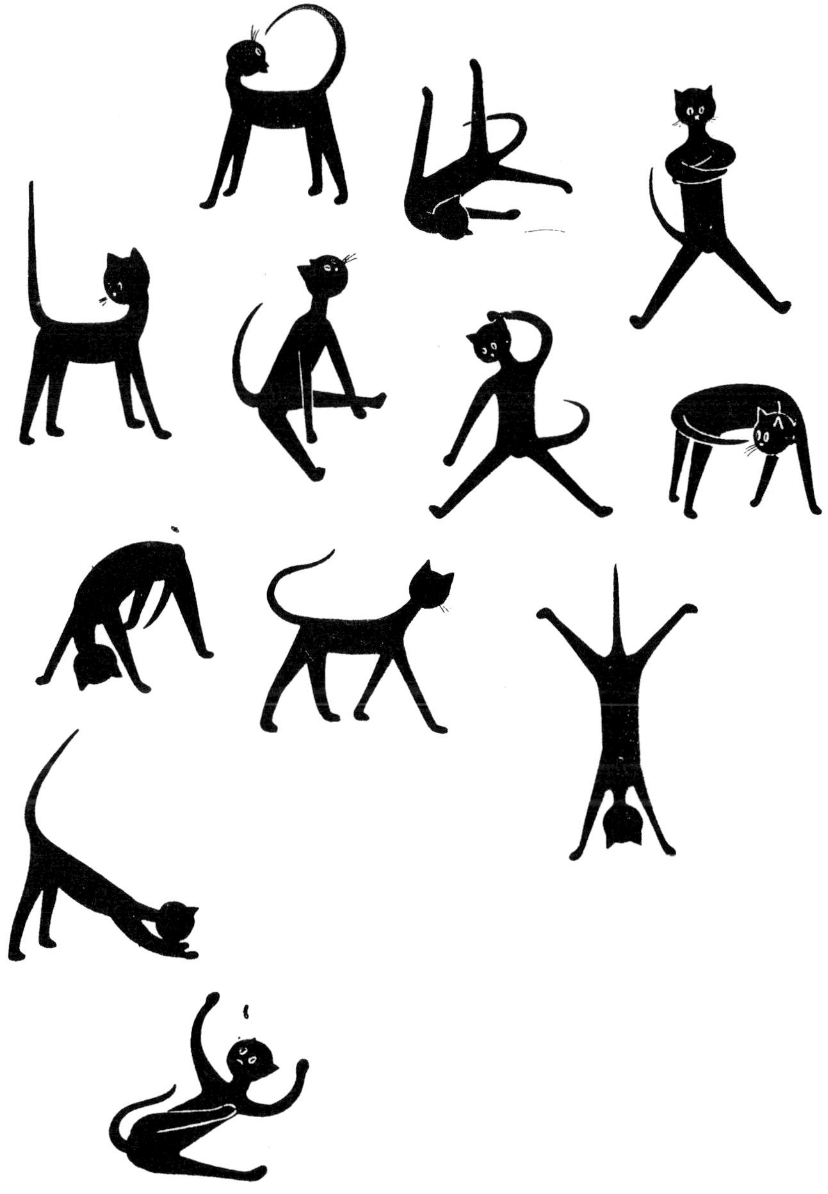

17 – Bruno Munari, *Meo Cat*, 1952

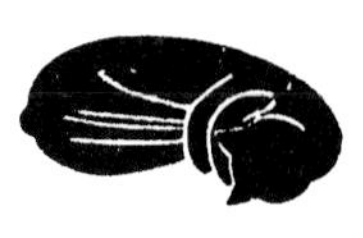

From now on, the design of the kitchen utensil must be based on the same principles as the pebble or the rock crystal, in other words, on those of simplicity (a sort of minimalism).

The factory must be isolated and placed at a distance from the town, which will be flooded with sun and air (void). The architect should even go so far as to gut areas which are too built-up; he must raze old buildings to the ground and whitewash the walls of brightly coloured houses.

Functionalism becomes the pretext of terrorism of the worst kind. Even if one wants to avoid frills and flourishes, preciosity and arabesques, is it really necessary to go to the extreme of iciness, and to rationalize such a destructive order?

The object remains trapped in the impasse, as does any other structure: indeed, it is precisely for fighting against the decoration or ornamentation which covered it that it destroys itself. Inevitably, the "self-punishing" architecture must lead to Post-Modernism.

The term "Post-Modernism" is used to refer to a rejection of hyper-functionalism, of dogmatic purism, of the cult of industry and of "shortage style." To a certain extent, it returns to the past and to tradition, and develops a form of architecture which resolutely mixes folklore and local (environmental) requirements.

Robert Venturi, in his book entitled *Ambiguity in Architecture*, advocates a coexistence of styles; he argues that this does not lead to confusion, but to enrichment and even to pleasure, justifying the presence of contrasts and contradictory features resulting from the "at the same time" principle. Mixtures and asynchronization are also viewed as being desirable. Whereas Bauhaus' "less is more" is firmly condemned, Venturi answers "more is not less" and even "less is a bore"!

Bauhaus' reaction to Art Nouveau's unbridled creativity gives way to Post-Modernism, which aims to counter its relentless suppressions.

Architecture in France, let us note, remains cartesian and attracted to "modernism," rejecting entangled or humorous designs. Indeed, the "Arche de la Défense," the Louvre Pyramid, the Ministry of Finances, the "Institut du Monde Arabe" and in particular the future Great Library (consisting in four square towers placed at right angles), all reflect a functionalist or purist credo, despite having been toned down here and there. Alterations have been made at times which may deceive one, but in fact, architecture continues to draw its fundamental inspiration from the same source as before.

And what about the "Centre Beaubourg"? Is it not a neo-baroque product of Post-Modernism? Is it a successful example of non-conformism, or on the contrary, is it yet another example of non-decorative architecture?

It appears that the architect has totally revolutionized form and has turned everything upside down; or rather, he has turned the monument "inside out": the "entrails" of the monument are placed on the outside, the interior becomes a space where connections are multiplied, movement is made easier, as well as possibilities of getting quickly anywhere (as Francis Ponge writes, it is not so much a monument but a *moviment*). Is it, then, a dream achievement of "hyper-design," has a reversal actually taken place?

I'm uncertain about the answer to this conclusive question. Given that the Centre favours mobility, and that the last remnants of privacy and convention have been abolished from this decided constructivism, one might be inclined to conceive of it as "meta-functional." This enormous suction and force pump—to use Francis Ponge's term yet again—is less like a refinery and more like a great heart muscle, which explains the coherence of this "mastodon." So, in fact, despite an apparently humorous intention, there is very little doubt as to the real nature of the monument.

Now, let us turn away from the Beaubourg Centre and from ultra-modernist Paris towards the object of everyday use. For it too, in the same way as the public buildings, wavers between the two extremes: either it is modular and bare, or it is baroque and over-ornamented.

It is pointless to argue that the field has shifted from the household object to architecture, since stylist, graphic designer, town planner, constructor, plastician and industrial "ideas man" are one and the same. The traditional dichotomy between painter and sculptor has already been put aside with good reason and sound evidence. Besides, Vasarely, amongst others, points in this direction: "The synthesis of the visual arts is a fait accompli, where the coordination of the different creative disciplines is concerned (painting, sculpture, architecture, town planning). At the same time, a philosophical synthesis is being elaborated. Painting and sculpture are becoming anachronistic terms: it would be better to speak of two- or three- or multi-dimensional plasticity.[7]"

So that one finds town planners who take an interest in utensils (bottles, boxes, coffee-grinders), and designers who apply themselves to the factory-made object as well as to the factory which produces them and which is in need of "re-making" or re-building. The city may be conceived of as a meta-achievement (or as a living-machine). The problem is the same in every field: to organize surfaces and volumes within a given space.

The major lesson is, however, that the past does not throw light on the proper path to follow: for it is involved in perpetual disputes and disappointing fluctuations.

Now, how may one avoid the fact that by styling an object, one distorts it? The whole operation is compromised from the start, given that one remains on the surface (packaging and presentation), without even attempting to dig down deeper: the only thing that counts is to increase sales (to seduce the helpless client). Raymond Loewy's photocopier, refrigerator and iron are all aerodynamic, giving the public what it wants (it is obsessed with speed and with breaking records). To this effect, he makes his appliances or vehicles lighter (he "deflates" them), eliminates any protruding parts, and rounds off the angles; most importantly, he hides the shameful mechanical parts (the motor especially) under a necessarily smooth, white sub-frame (not so much for hygienic reasons but to give an immaculate touch to the whole).

Raymond Loewy's formula: "the most beautiful curve is that of increasing sales" is a cynical reflection of the deviating path, which this graphic artist has taken, who favours conceptions which are simple, but above all which are meant to entice. The question is whether the object is being "saved" or enriched in this way, or whether, on the contrary, it is being alienated to the mercantile system. It becomes two pieces of merchandise in one, and it is the surrounding marketing layer which overwhelms all the rest.

Ultimately, there does not seem to be any solution to the problem: if nothing is added to the common utensil, it is reduced to its necessarily disappointing shell (its utilitarian aspect crushes all the rest). If, on the

(7) — Vasarely, *Plasticité*, Casterman, Tournai, 1970, p. 124.

other hand, it is decorated or even slightly ornamented (an emblem), the result is a beautiful lie. Added to which the unity of the object is shattered and its sound simplicity lost. Can this aporia be resolved in any way?

The question, however, whether art is really able to lower itself to the extent of penetrating the most humble and most pathetic forms of materiality, such as an electric shaver, a bottle or a simple coffee-pot, arises once more. Can it possibly be accomodated by that which it has dismissed for so long?

***

The object is thus torn asunder and trapped in a both historical and theoretical impasse (kitsch, from *kitschen*: to blotch, whereby the ornamental design only serves to conceal defects, operating in fraudulent manner, and thereby depraving the object still further—threatens to take over). Who will come to its rescue?

The only possible way out is to look at the proposals contained in certain monographies on the subject of "domestic aesthetics."

I do not claim to be writing a history of design, nor to be awarding prizes for the best designs. I have, however, chosen a few achievements as examples of how to avoid all the aforementioned errors. The problem is not a matter for historians—even though it is useful to recall the recent past—but for theorists of innovation. In short, how may one reject a strictly functional approach without falling into the trap of pretty-prettiness or preciosity in plastic design?

Let us begin with Bruno Munari (born in 1907), a "relatively forgotten" Italian designer. Italy has always been and still is the centre of renewal. "Neo-design" ("progetto") and Post-Modernism have flourished there, advocating playfulness, surprise and sometimes derision as opposed to strict (northern) functionalism. It is here that *Alchimia* was launched in 1977, followed by *Memphis* in 1981 by Ettore Sottsass, "the guru of Memphis." In Milan (as in other Italian cities), a school has also been founded, the Domus Academy (Mendini, Branzi), the structures of which stipulate: "There is no difference between a spoon and a city, given that the latter is indeed definable as a set of spoons."

Why Italy? Its industrialists (Olivetti, Fiat, Montedison) have understood the importance of collaboration between the producer and the ideas man. It is also in Italy that Futurism really took off (reconciling art with machines, change, and modernity) all the more enthusiastically given that the fascist régime has constrained and overseen production in the past, as well as the city plastic arts (art, monuments, the city itself).

Be that as it may, Munari who was a follower of the Futurist movement (his "useless machines" were an early example of imagination applied to mechanics) worked at bridging the gaps between art and the public and took to producing factory-made objects (in 1948, he founded the "concrete art" movement). Enough of purely biographical details! What do we owe him?

He has managed to overcome the central antinomy, by simply opening the object up, by digging into it and thereby forcing it to reveal its diverse components (buried inside)—rather than artificially plastering a decoration onto the object's exterior (thus turning it into a mere frame), rather than imposing a metaphoric meaning on it. He realizes that to "tattoo" the object is pointless when it is possible instead to uncover its surprisingly plural dimensions. Thus, one avoids, on the one hand, producing uniform objects, and on the other, the fuss of superimposing an extra layer on it!

Henceforth, the multiple may inhabit unity: Munari received the "Compasso d'oro" (the national reward for designers) for his little flexible monkeys made out of reinforced rubber, and which are able to adopt any position (1953). In the previous year, he had designed his *Meo Cat* (1952). (see fig. 17)

This lightweight object can be easily transformed and put back together again. It is, as it were, what one makes of it: it has no essence since it can be changed in an instant (it is both solid and fluid at the same time).

Kinetic art had not come this far, since it dealt with a structure which was mobile from the start, and ready to spring to life at any moment, whenever touched the slightest breeze, as in Calder's art. Here, on the contrary, it is an extremely solid and rigid structure which is activated.

For the best defence of this art, let us consult René Thom's theory of catastrophies: "Aesthetics is a morphological science," he writes, "it deals with objects which, in the case of the visual arts (painting, sculpture), are material, or else purely musical (music, poetry). From this point of view, aesthetics is superior to many of the social sciences, such as psychology or sociology, for they are totally incapable of defining their objects in space.[8]"

He then adds: "There is one essential difference, however, between aesthetics and a morphological science, and that is that aesthetics excludes repetition. Each and everyone of its objects is a hapax, and all copies are immediately dismissed from its field of study.[9]"

Thom conceives the work of art, which is very close to topology, in terms of the interplay between contour and fragment.

The first thing required is its concentration within a specific area (within the frame). Only then may there emerge a conflict between the different possible leading elements (arising from the discovery of other centres or influential areas). Another way of apprehending the work of art is to see it in terms of the struggle between form and force: "Form is visible, but, in principle, static. Force, on the other hand, is invisible, but it sometimes produces effects which are both dynamic and visible.[10]"

Munari's toys (a thriving industry) are a good illustration as well as a confirmation of this original definition of the work of art. He also advocated other similar types of operation and manipulation: for instance, he produces objects made out of light cardboard or synthetic fibre—his travel sculptures—which can be reversed or altered in one way or another, giving rise to a constantly changing (and portable) environment.

The principle of stability (as well as the traditional heaviness of the object) are called into question by the ability of these sculptures to switch from one state to another so easily.

Flexy (1968) is another such example, where steel wires allow for a whole series of permutations. Some might argue that these are mere games. This flexible wire-netting, however, enables one to create new shapes, and thanks to the multiple possibilities which are thus engendered, one learns to view the world differently.

Lastly, let us not forget the various materials and carpets which change colour when touched or trodden upon (1986). A number of

(8) — René Thom, *Apologie du Logos*, Hachette, Paris, 1990, p. 105.
(9) — Id. p. 105.
(10) — Id. p. 132.

Italian designers, including Denis Santachiara[11], have used this achievement (interactivity) in their own work: a red dress, for example, which turns green according to the outside temperature. A single object— no matter how common (cloth)—can be plural at the same time, down to its very core, not just superficially (hence the slimmering scarf, shawl or tie).

The dream object contains a number of potential shapes within it, which appear mainly, for instance, when concave forms are inverted and become convex: in no time at all, at a toss of a die, it turns into something else, or into its opposite. In order to achieve this, one must rotate, substitute one part for another, compress or extend it: in short, it requires one to go "transformation-mad." Plurality is thus accomodated in the utensil, which is no longer reduced to being monotonously static. The way was certainly paved by the so-called "Gestaltpsychologie," but the latter stressed the way one visualizes things to the exclusion of anything else (optical ambivalence). The designer's project, on the other hand, is more ambitious: to produce objects of daily use which, beneath their façade, have a multimorphic potential (the different arrangements). By doing so, he attempts to reveal the supernatural dimension of the object itself, without appealing to outside factors for help.

Let us now turn from an Italian designer to an American (from California), who is both an architect and a designer—the two disciplines being indistinct, as far as I am concerned. My task is to find a "solution" to an apparently insoluble problem: the unification of function with that which goes beyond it—without weakening the object or covering it with excessive detail!

What is Frank O. Gehry's proposal, and how does he overcome the antinomy? What is the nature of the art he introduces into the most ordinary furniture?

One cannot help being struck by his furniture, which is made out of corrugated cardboard. With a roll, he is able to produce armchairs, chairs, tables, and other pieces of "supporting" furniture. Even Bloomingdale's, the department store, has commercialized them, and twenty years on, they are still in use.

---

(11) — I have devoted only a few lines to Denis Santachiara in the present text in order not to repeat what I have already written in my article on him: "Santachiara ha glorificato la merce," in *Santachiara, l'Estetica dell'uso*, Reggio Emilia, 1990. It is to Pasquale Alferi and to his extraordinary knowledge of Italian culture that I owe my discovery of the importance and the variety of design in Milan and in the rest of Italy.

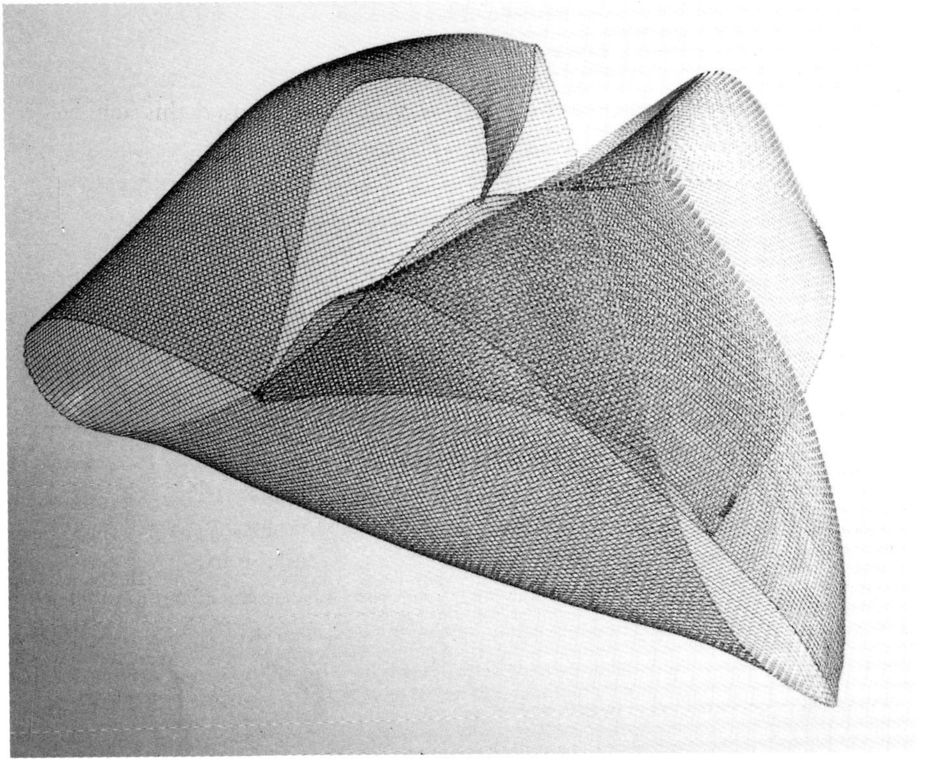

18 – Bruno Munari, *Concave, convex*, 1947

His furniture is the result of a happy, wonderful combination of unity (the generating idea) and multiplicity (the product itself). Furthermore, each strip of cardboard is wavy and creased, its ends may be stuck together, whilst it remains slightly detached from its neighbouring strips. In general, when two processes are involved, it leads to failure. Either one overwhelms the other, and the result bears witness to the domination of the former, or else, when both processes are equally important, the accent is placed on the plurality of means, so that it becomes impossible to establish any order; the result is a jumble, and even a chaos, at times.

In this case, however, it is the very unity—no extra element has been added—which gives way to the most varied multiplicity.

So that it appears that the seat made of cardboard strips has managed to avoid the trap into which creation usually falls, whereby one either lapses into monotony, or into over-abundance. Here, it is always the same thing which generates creation, but it is a flexible material, able both to be straightened out or to be curved or creased; it is unrolled in the same way as a pastry. Modular creations cannot be rolled up in this manner because the rigidity of tubes or elements inhibit it. Gehry's work, on the other hand, takes advantage in an unexpected way of the flexibility and "rollability" of his material which is both hard and soft (he uses almost "wrinkled" cardboard to produce an armchair).

Need one be reminded that all seats are, by definition, the result of the criss-crossing of lines and surfaces, which either intersect or diverge? In the present instance, however, everything is inscribed in a continuum: the geometric model or structure no longer prevails (a new morphogenesis: the act of unrolling).

Furthermore, the slightly unlevel position of the strips is an important factor conveying upon the seat a "corduroy" effect. The undulating surface is not totally smooth.

Also, the edges of the seat are far from being totally vertical; on the contrary, they finish off in "accordeon-style," the aim being to avoid a lump of volume, a right angle, or anything that might recall a sharp edge. The latter is substituted for a gentle rolling effect, a regular cascade of independent parts designed nonetheless to fit into each other when the time comes. This sequence of parts demonstrates both their (relative) independence, and their (designed) closeness.

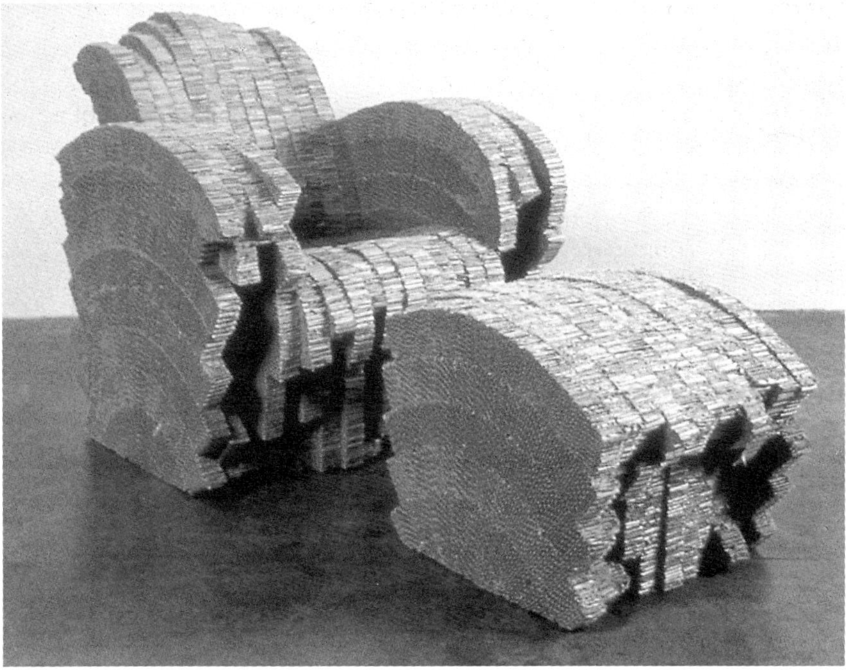

19 – Frank O. Ghery, *Cardboard Furniture*

The inventor thus achieves a synthesis, whereby a fluid, transformational process gives rise to solid and stable "form." The result is a rich and ungeometric object, obtained nonetheless by a single method: casting or fashioning. These folds and meanders, this sinuous creamy paste—which might be yellow—is most appealing. The fascination, however, lies less in the final result than in the impression one has of perceiving the very process at work in the object (as if it were still being casted: the object should not be perceived as a contiguous result, but as a continuum).

Let us point out that Frank O. Gehry was chosen to build the "Vitra Design Museum." Vitra, the German company, which manufactures furniture (in particular office seats and chairs) has a collection of the most original pieces in this field: it is said to have collected up to one thousand two hundred of them, both antique and modern examples (including those of Eames and Nelson, of Sottsass, Kuramata and Santachiara). After having decided to exhibit them in a Museum of Design, Vitra commissioned Gehry to plan and build it: he proposed to build a complex where snow would be the dominant theme. It would have been pointless to construct a Californian-style building in Germany, or so he felt; the aim was to adapt it to a country where it is winter during much of the year; hence a complex which would be flooded by light and by dazzling whiteness.

Gehry was also asked to elaborate an enormous receptacle (a seat) which would contain all invented forms of seating. Why not turn from the contents to the container?

And yet, Gehry owes his fame not so much to his armchairs or chairs, but to all the buildings he has inspired, in the United States and in Europe. The *Vila Olimpica* in Barcelona (planned for the 1992 Olympic Games) is one of them.

The aim of the architect (a post-modernist if there ever was one) was to gently ease into the space destined for his building. He wanted to refrain from subjecting it to the usual mistreatment (as is testified by all those giant sky-scrapers, tower-blocks and heights, generally). Given that Barcelona's activity is turned towards the sea, on which it is built, it seemed most appropriate to construct an enormous vessel, a hull, or rather a great big fish, devoid of head, tail, fins or scales. Naturally, it would be placed on metallic pillars, designed to support it.

Lighting had already incorporated "aerial fish" as well as snake forms. Here, however, it represents a sort of undulating, creeping paradigm, or even a standard for the anti-geometric movement (including neither spheres, nor cylinders, nor any orthogonal shapes). The fact that the tail-end is raised above the rest ensures that the complex does not appear to have been made of one piece; it looks asymmetrical (from the outside); its parts have been arranged gradationally. It succeeds to avoid both a "messy" effect and traditional rectilinearity.

Most importantly, however, this golden, aerial fish, the most primitive and sacred of all beings, is a celebration of the symbolic order. Gehry does not neglect its role (it is meant to contrast with the neighbouring hotel-tower, and to balance it out by correcting its rigidity), neither does he attempt to subdue the light reflected by its shiny texture, rather he allows it to sparkle (as if it had sticky scales).

Finally, he has not sacrificed its cultural aspect to its utilitarian function: until now, all too often, the modern object was defined by the economy of its component parts and by its function. Here, although, these considerations have not been totally dismissed, it is the allegorical or metaphoric aspect of the object (its meaning) which is stressed.

The fish is the concrete symbol of vigorous movement, agility and swiftness: by appealing to it, one does away with all heaviness, as well as the tendency to fill space up with ridiculous volumes, under pretext of simplicity and rigour. The innovation, then, consists in the lightness of the structure: all excess and fuss have been avoided.

The vessel contains, encloses, swallows up (the Jonas complex), just as it is engulfed in turn by the sea: it is both content and container.

Without wishing to go into any biographical details, it is usually the case that passionate motivation springs from life itself. If it were not for a particular motivating event, the builder or creator would lack inventive energy. Now, by means of this immense and fantastic ichtyoid vessel, is Gehry (born Goldberg) not reactualizing the Jewish culture with which he is familiar, a culture which grants fish a privilege? Judaism considers all beasts impure and prohibits the drinking of their blood, and, at the same time, it blames the slaughterer who must bleed the animal, whereas fish, on the contrary, is considered a neutral food, like the egg, and does not provoke the same anxiety.

On a more elementary level, fish do not require special treatment, nor to be raised, given that they multiply endlessly. No wonder it is a symbol of fertility and vitality—and no wonder it was deemed a gift from God to destitute man! In a word, it belongs to the dream or even religious world by virtue of being filled to the brim with meaning.

Now Spain, a land of Christianity and a maritime nation is a most obvious and deserving candidate for this kind of zoomorphic architecture: one need not turn to astrological considerations, nor to psychoanalytic theories (the phallic symbol) to see why. The Judeo-Christian tradition is sufficient explanation for a type of architecture which does not exclude collective imagination. Athletes would also approve of this consecration of a symbol of strength (the fish, which inhabits the bottom of the ocean, draws its energizing and redemptive power from it).

Frank O. Gehry is said to have answered in an interview on his return to archaism: "Post-Modernists seek their references in the past, so why not go still further back in time, back to oceanic prehistory? Why not go all the way back to the dawn of time, to the time of heroes?"

But is it not nature, precisely, which is supplying him with his "generating image" or his model? Barcelona's enormous ichtyoid container, it must be conceded, has renounced the attributes pointing to marine existence: towering above one is only a schematic and free form. The architect may have been inspired by the fish, but this does not mean that he has sought to imitate it.

The designer—the rhythmic succession of concave and convex forms betrays his work on corrugated cardboard—arrives at a synthesis between minimalism and suppleness. He has managed to eliminate both quintessential form and embellishments or complications from his work.

The investigation of other "centres" or buildings would lead to the same result: in each case, one would find that the symbolic and the functional merge; unity is not shattered and decoration is kept to a minimum.

In most cases, Post-Modernism reacts much too strongly against modernism and it shows: a thing and its opposite boil down to the same thing. Gehry, on the contrary, leads the way towards Post-Modernism in its real and serene sense.

***

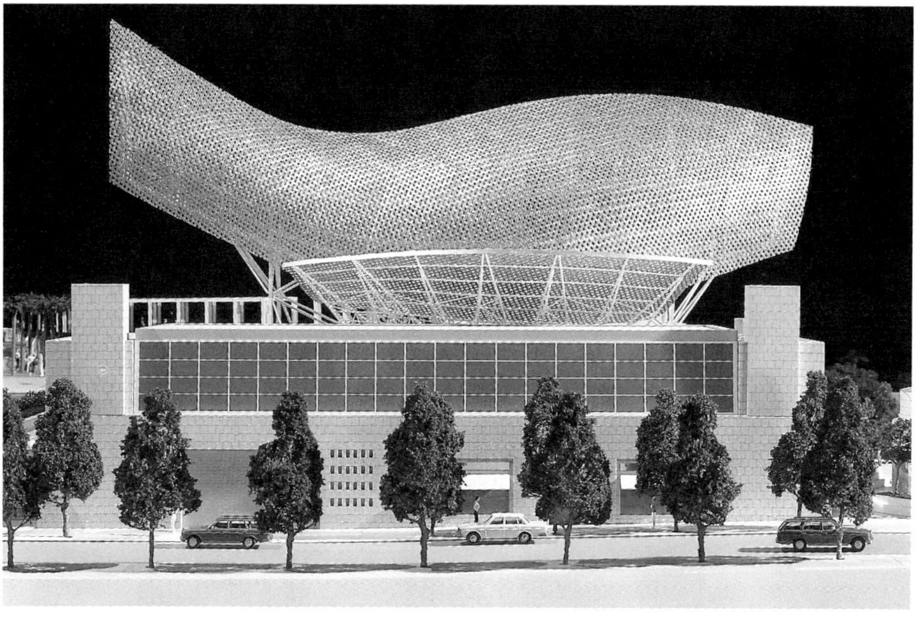

20 – Frank O. Ghery, *Vila Olimpica*, 1992 (© J. Scott Smith)

In this overview, I intentionally adopt an experimental, or even technical and scientific point of view in order to throw light upon the ingenious way in which some have taken up the challenge, avoiding well-known traps, such as facileness or simple reaction to past trends. Now, what is so daring about their work?

The Frenchman Philippe Starck deserves special attention, although the decision is admittedly arbitrary and subject to limitations.

It would have been just as appropriate to concentrate on Nouvel, Garouste, Dubuisson, Putman, Villmotte, as well as on the creations of other German, Belgian, Japanese, Dutch or Finnish designers—but I do not claim to be writing a History of design. My task is merely to highlight a few "solutions" to this mountain of a problem. It would also have been possible to draw up a list of obvious failures, but what is the point of entering into dispute?

I shall attempt to analyse, instead, one or two of Philippe Starck's greatest successes, and especially that which he has baptized *Ray Menta* (see fig. 21). This refers to a desk-light which is unusual both in practical terms, and in terms of its design, for Starck has eliminated all visible electric wires, the bulb, which gives off a shaft of light, and the switch, which requires pressing. These attributes, which are too reminiscent of a candle, have disappeared, and have given way to a slight, inclined plate which emits a fluorescent light. No more source, no more cord!

To "switch it on," all that is needed is to touch it slightly, or to stroke it gently, just as if one were dealing with a "pet animal"; soon, its owner will only need to walk into the room, and *Ray Menta* will spread light automatically: the responses of this most obliging object will be controlled by an electronic device, activated by the person's arrival.

Starck himself explained his *Ray Menta* in terms of a general theory of prosthesis, his aim being to bridge the gap between man and his environment. He sees the automobile as a pair of artificial legs, the calculator as an artificial brain, the tape-recorder as an artificial auditory-memory aid. Until now, man has been able to project his body onto the outside world, now it is time for the reverse to occur: the outside must be allowed to reflect its fundamental abilities onto man.

Starck aims not only to bring man closer to his objects, but he also expresses openly the desire that he interiorize them—this is what he calls the "pace-maker aesthetics"—within a general and integrated bio-mechanical system.

The extreme limit has been reached by what Starck calls "magic design": the distance between the lamp, which is activated by a slight touch, and the body, is narrowed. For the object, until now, had stood opposite us ("ob-" meaning "against"), displaying its hard, heavy and even foreign quality.

Why the name *Ray Menta*? Starck answers: "*Ray* as in sun-ray and *Menta* as in mental: it sends a stream of light which cuts through the mists, thus helping the mind to work."

Ray Menta, however, resembles a fish (the "ray") more than anything else. Its pisciform aspect confers upon it an animal appearance (the animal object) and evokes the rapid movement of fish, like that of light, which reaches man at high speed.

The word "Ray" is (deliberately?) confusing: it may well refer to the ray of sun, but it also belongs to zoological vocabulary. It distinguishes, amongst selachians, between the Mobula family (devils of the sea) and the Manta family (mantis of the sea). Now, both belong to the torpedo group (electric rays and all other torpedos). So that despite the "a" in Manta having been replaced by the "e" in mental, this shared electric quality leads one to draw parallels (and if not their electric quality, then it is the shape itself of the prototype which leads one to do so: a wide plate which can be positioned obliquely). It should also be noted that these Manta rays may attain the weight of up to two tons and a width of seven meters (giant Manta). Starck must be thrilled to swim back up to the surface from the depths of our amazing ocean, in order to bring light to a room. The shared electric quality and form, then, explain the shared terminology, as well as the comparison between the marine animal and the mechanical zoomorphic object. And finally, they also justify the comparison between the carnal and smooth appearance of both the animal and the object.

The diffusor can be placed on a desk equipped with so-called "shark-fins," thus reconstituting the fluid universe of an immense and turbulent ocean.

This light, an example of inventive "Neo-Design," has been altered slightly: the glowing plate, instead of being uniform all over, is now made up of a grid with openings, reminiscent of shutters: in this way, the effect of "daybreak," filtering through the parallel strips of the shutters, is created.

However, generally speaking, Starck, the baroque theoretician of biomechanics, does not deny that his object is still divided by an inner conflict and torn between two opposite requirements: lines and surfaces are no longer at its origin (as in the old system), and it tends to avoid the usual heaviness and stability assigned to it by its function. Starck, on the contrary, strives to breathe lightness and weightlessness into it, thereby creating a magic and unreal effect.

This is not the same as disguising the necessary functionalism of the object with fancy accessories—a disastrous duality! —, since every layer, including the utilitarian, must equally contribute to its take off.

"That is why I have worked on creating a "flying lamp," [...] why I have attempted to create things which have come slightly unstuck from reality, by stressing their instability, and the tensions which run through them. I have made Mitterrand's armchair, for instance, the *Richard III*, entirely out of calibrated aluminium, which was built by a helicopter constructor, just because I wanted to create a paradoxical piece of furniture, in that by definition, furniture is heavy.[12]"

Paradoxical is perhaps not the right word; "contradictory" is more appropriate. Indeed, all objects stand on their base, or on their legs: "The fourth leg of a chair is superfluous," says Philippe Starck; "the tripod creates a tension. The spirit of a three-legged seat is obviously quite different. [...] An incipient relationship is established with the person who is going to sit in it.[13]"

The following statement is quite revealing: "Gravity is something we experience daily, without even noticing, so that weightlessness is one of the most magical, mysterious and enchanting things. That is the reason why I have worked on the flying lamp and why I have made inflatable furniture.[14]"

Ray Menta is rectangular and it lies, precisely, on its smallest side. One could not hope to find a smaller base; there is no better way to confer

(12) — Talks dating from 1987, Christine Colin, *Philippe Starck*, Pierre Mardaga, Liège, 1989, pp. 243, 257.

(13) — Id., p. 257. The "ideas man" must at all costs take the function, balance, fixity of the object into account, but he also wants to create an effect of surprise and above all to reduce its heaviness and its immobility, by "uplifting" it.

(14) — Id., p. 243.

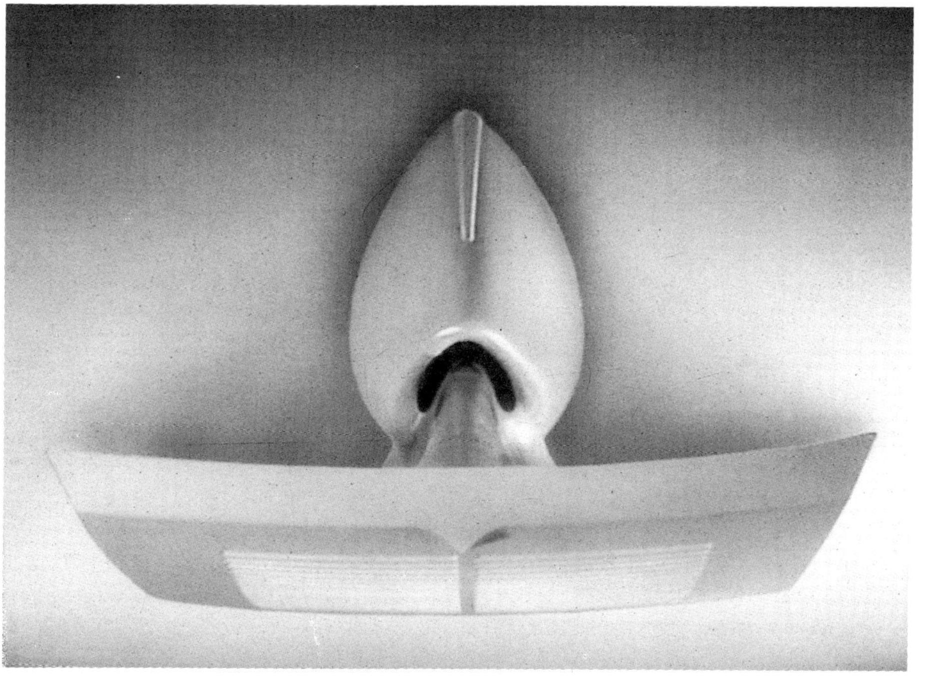

21 – Philippe Starck, *Ray Menta*, 1984 (prototype)

upon it a quasi-levitational appearance: when in oblique position, the extreme thinness of the flat surface adds to the effect.

There is a second essential operative fact in Starck's work which needs pointing out: mobility has virtually been made possible with this ray. True, the object itself does not move, but it diffuses light rapidly at the slightest touch. Its lightness is a liberating factor; surely, one day, one will truly invent a way for it to genuinely move through the room (an aerial ray).

Indeed, most of Starck's furniture is already mobile and multivalent, such as his chair, which in an instant can be transformed into a tea table, by folding down the backrest. From now on, then, "form follows fold."

Some of Starck's other achievements include a cupboard which can be turned into a writing case, a sofa with a flap, an armchair with a parasol, a lamp which is also a coat-hanger, etc.

In the eighteenth century, cabinet-makers had already made multiple furniture, such as the stool which, by being turned upside down, became a chair, the secretaire which was easily turned into a desk, etc. But never before have transfigurative mutations been taken this far. The "same" could only be transformed into something similar—there is not such a great difference between the stool and the chair as one may imagine: the role of both is to support and to carry. In the present case, however, much more is achieved than a simple nest of tables or clever disappearing and reappearing acts: an object can now be folded in any possible way, like in the case of a "swing-wing" table.

It is the combination of the desire to greatly reduce their weight and the desire to respect their function which has given rise to this type of furniture. Furthermore, the fact that a same unit can have various different usages means that it is relatively indeterminate, thus spelling the end of the old relation between mean and result, which was both strict and burdensome. The fact that a utensil is bestowed with plural dimensions is a relief and a liberation, rescueing one from functionalism.

***

It might well be that I have chosen Bruno Munari, Frank O. Gehry and Philippe Starck—the reversible object, the symbolic and the biomechanical, or even the toy, the collective vessel and the pisciform lamp—for subjective reasons; nonetheless, I have taken note of how they have rendered commonplace objects aesthetic by creating an original morphology: the outright success of Post-Modernism (understood as genuine, non-reactional, non-aggressive, non-violent, non-excessive, non-theatrical), and the triumph of these ingenious devices. New materials, supple, light and resistant at the same time, have enabled innovation in each case (where the designer has chosen to use old materials, such as corrugated cardboard, he renews it by extending its use).

All three have managed to avoid the failure that springs from trivialized industrial rationalism (tubular structures), without going to the other extreme of designing things which are contorted or incoherent. The resulting "objects" are varied and playful, imaginative and magic.

But is it really appropriate to speak of art in this context: amongst table sets, armchairs, and even possibly automobiles? Is spiritual experience not being confused here with pleasure and convenience?

The same question crops up time and time again, due to the fact that academic and traditional art relies on exclusion solely. "Poor art" (*l'arte povera*) had already attempted to rehabilitate "materials" which purism had eliminated for the sake of more noble, durable, and therefore richer materials, such as precious wood, marble, gold leaf and copper. A struggle was needed before rusty, cracked, dented, mended, creased materials (in other words what has been called junk culture, the culture of waste if not of dustbins) could be accepted into "the circle of beauty." Dubuffet himself, one should not forget, sang the praises of dirty oil, crushed materials, "the gravel on the ground," and debris.

Similarly, why dismiss the ordinary or the prosaic object? Why oppose oneself to a domo-aesthetics which makes place for dishes, pans and cutlery?

Religion (the meal) does not shy away from it. Paul Claudel made this happy remark: "The family table is not a trough, but a kind of altar, aspiring to more than the mere satisfaction of our animal needs. I was horrified to witness, in certain cheap American restaurants, those so-called plates, which are divided up into compartments, a relic no doubt of the emigrant's or the trapper's billy can. The client is treated like a pig and is served his bellyful all in one go.[15]"

So it is not surprising that what has been legitimately called "the art of the table" should follow next.

(15) — Paul Claudel, *Oeuvres en prose*, Bibliothèque de la Pléiade, Paris, 1965, p. 359.

By choosing the environment, the habitat, the street or the body as a medium and a surface, Body Art and Land Art have shown the way. So why not include the glass, the fork or the chair? Some may retort that they belong to the applied arts, but is there such a thing as an art which is not applied? Art once served the cause of religion and everything sacred; then it turned to grand themes, to exploits; it served as a memory-aid and it even helped one to appreciate that which was often overlooked. To pursue its radiant expansion, it needs to renew everyday life by penetrating into the most banal or familiar objects.

The analysis of Stella's works in particular revealed that "installation-works" were the animus behind modern art, so too, the very similar "art of window-dressing" is the impetus behind this new art-form, which can be found in useful or commercialized objects and which is not far off from the universe of the hardware store or the market.

Léger agreed with this point of view: "The street has become a permanent spectacle of increasing intensity [...] The display-window spectacle has become a major source of anxiety in the retailer's activity [...] Can you yourself doubt the extreme care that goes into preparing these displays?[16]"

A few lines further down, he even goes so far as to claim the shop-keeper's superiority over the famous artist or painter: "[...] this worthy craftsman, forging his own work with difficulty and conscientiousness, which is more valuable than those expensive canvases; they are going to disappear, but he will have to renew his work in a few days with the same care and the same keenness. Men like this, such artisans, incontestably have a concept of art—one closely tied to commercial purposes, but one that is a plastic achievement of a new order and the equivalent of existing artistic manifestations, whatever they may be."

Besides, is there any famous artist who has not, at one time or another, applied himself to posters, advertisements, to creating furniture or bibelots? In March 1962, Mathieu, the painter, wrote in the catalogue of an exhibition devoted to the object: "From the Merovingians to the Renaissance, from Louis XIV to the eighteenth century and even up until 1900, the shape of a carriage, the curves of a carriage entrance and the design of a brooch all had similar features. They may have made up a particular

(16) — Fernand Léger, "The Machine Aesthetics: the Manufactured Object, The Artisan and the Artist" in *Functions of Painting*, The Viking Press, New York, 1973, p. 56.

style, as a result, but in the first instance, they reflected a meeting-point between the artist's conception of beauty and the craftsman's idea of it, when it was not the artist himself who executed or overlooked the execution of the work."

At this exhibition, thirty-two artists (including Calder, Ernst, Picasso, Tanguy and Dubuffet) put on show, amongst other things, the jewelry they had designed. The collaboration between the plastician and the manufacturer (or the contemporary industrialist) is undeniable then, even though it had been neglected or passed under silence.

It is from this perspective that the designer, the artist of the commonplace object, the specialist in "domo-aesthetics," the interior architect are being challenged to create new forms and to reinvent even the most minor utensils and everything around us which we use. Aristotle said that the gods also inhabited the kitchen. Art has joined them.

CONCLUSION

I have analysed two separate trends which converge, and finally meet. This was inevitable, given the great number of artists who have participated in domestic-industrial transformation (furniture, chairs, ceramics, jewelry). Some of them, not necessarily minor ones, have gone a little further and have applied themselves to road signals, to polychromatic walls or factories, to fabrics and their designs.

Among these artists is Vasarely, who has spoken outright in favour of the fusion of the two movements that we have been discussing. He writes: "the produce of art extends from the pleasant utilitarian object to art for art's sake, from the agreeable to the transcendant. The whole field of plastic activities is inscribed within a vast hierarchical world: decorative arts, fashion, advertising and propaganda through images, the decors of industry events, celebrations, sporting events, theatre scenery, [...] and finally, the quest for an authentic avant-garde.[1]"

Admittedly, the rising trend (design) is rather slim, but nonetheless it works towards renewing that which has been neglected until now, and integrates it into a general aesthetics.

The common features of these two movements are their "inscriptional" passion (the carrying out of the act), their desire to alter a threatened environment (the city), the will to fight discrimination (why reject objects of daily use?), to put an end to lies and old conventions, their belief in the necessity of invention (not to content oneself with what has now become academism), their calling into question of the pictorial act, their taste for assemblage and montage.

***

But this is not always conceded by critics, who refer to contemporary art in caustic fashion, judging it to be too dispersed and therefore impossible to grasp.

(1) — Vasarely, *Plasticité*, Casterman/poche, Tournai, 1970, p.133.

The only task I have set myself has been to map out this area, recognizing indeed the existence of many byways, a dense maze of intertwining paths: the truth of the matter is nonetheless that, when these are seen from a height or from afar, one observes that they all lead towards a given centre, just as the many different tracks in a natural landscape all converge towards a town or a city.

It is my belief that I have managed to locate the "focal point" of this muddled network, and have done so by concentrating in the main on the attractions presented by this centre, to which most trajectories or circuits lead—this does not, however, exclude other ways of moving about, strolling, or escaping this network.

Given that I have only gone down a few of these paths, it is easy to claim that I have not given a full account of things. But my priority was to draw out the spirit of the whole, as well as the problems to which it is confronted, and some of the exemplary solutions which have been suggested. It was only natural that anti-aporetic strategies should override the analysis of plasiticity. In short, I have devoted myself less to describing an aesthetics than to a methodology (method comes from the Greek *odos*, meaning path).

I am well aware that one may have many reservations on the subject, and also that the apotheosis of that which is banal is by no means a recent trend.

But let us give up the panoramic point of view in order to take a "close-up" look at things. For one will see that "the still life" of the classical period neither really appealed to, nor celebrated the ordinary object; rather, it was represented as a vanity and expressed the frailty of goods. Often, a skull or a candle on the point of becoming extinguished are placed on the dining-room table or next to a bouquet of flowers. All is apparently peaceful, and seems to give rise to serenity, but in fact, all is threatened and unstable.

One might want to argue that Chardin celebrated the banal object, but in fact his recognition of it was not real, it was symbolic. His work is a calm and self-confident defence of the austere and hardworking, provincial petty bourgeoisie: he depicts its humble occupations, the seriousness betrayed by its gestures, as well as its moral spirit (a mother is seen to reprimand a distracted little girl who has botched her embroidery; another brushes off her son's clothes before he goes to school). The dining-room is always kept neat and tidy. It contains neither Bohemian crystal, nor fan, nor even shiny dishes. Chardin was brought up in poor surroundings (his father was a carpenter), a world apart from the frivolous and affected aristocracy. So his painting is related to social criticism. The object is a pretext to teach a lesson; if not, it is a disguised threat; it will only be recognized much later, once art has liberated itself from the rules and limits of classical pictoriality (the illusionist projection of perception). Neither Chardin's caldron, nor his bowl of fruit; neither the tree of the School of Barbizon, nor the Impressionists' beach were able to achieve the "break" which led to the substitution of representation for presentation.

I have not been afraid, it must be said, to define art as the discovery of technical solutions, or of new arrangements. Dismissing the current dramatizing attitudes towards art, I have even gone so far as to compare the artist with the artisan: whilst the former draws his inspiration from a basic structure or from any constraining factor, the latter executes a montage unknown yet, which he effects victoriously and which provokes wonder due to the effect of surprise.

***

A more incisive objection is also raised against the contemporary art world, namely that the existence of a flourishing industry is undeniable, creating fashions, launching artists, causing prices to soar and corrupting the market. It is useless, therefore, to ramble on about art when it is the fruit of such an incredible "market place process" in which thousands of participants are involved. Today's hero is forgotten tomorrow, and the critic who praises him to the sky will in turn be the butt of ridicule.[2]

Let us turn back to Ready-Made art which undoubtedly gave rise,

(2) — I do not agree with Anne Cauquelin's brilliant and fascinating analysis (*l'Art contemporain*, Que sais-je?, Paris, 1992) on contemporary art and on those who originated it (Marcel Duchamp, Andy Warhol). According to her, modern artists have abolished beauty, uniqueness in art, and even taste; they have set up a vast (international) network, an enormous system which brings together producers and consumers, but places the real deciders between the two: the critics, magazines, wheeler-dealers, art gallery owners, collectors, sellers, in other words, a mass of professionals.

pioneered even, the playing of hoaxes. As the ancestor of all sort of descendant movements, it seems to have succeeded totally in an unprecedented disappearing-act, an illusion in the second degree.

Indeed, critics consider something to be a work of art, understood as something which is arranged and mysterious, only if it satisfies the four strange requirements:

a) The initial object may be anything at all. Arbitrariness sets in from the start.

b) An artist seizes it, invests it, and even signs it.

c) The members of the public are invited to repeat this "empty formula," which is all the more easy for them to do, and which they do with all the more zeal, given that they are taken aback by the incomprehensibility of it all. Is it not the truth that they feel put out and even guilty for not understanding?

d) The instituted museum and other exhibiting or sales galleries ratify the contract or the "near-agreement" with the public. The trick has worked! It leads to the triumph of the coffee-grinder, the lemon-squeezer or the kettle, and the audience's captivation!

Of course, none of the above four are in the least bit founded:

a) The reason for choosing, amongst the many possible banal objects, a bicycle wheel or a urinal is precisely because these are the funniest and craziest, the aim being to surprise the audience.

b) The artist signs it with his name or with a pseudonym in order, precisely, to stress the comical side of the operation (Marcel Duchamp inscribed the name R. Mutt on a urinal, turned upside-down, and entitled *Fountain*).

c) One needs to condition the public in order to manipulate it easily. The museum, in the meantime, an objective accomplice, ratifies the hoax.

Art reflects this society (of communication and consumerism) whilst creating it at the same time (it goes around in circles). In itself, it is constituted of signs which circulate, it is redundant, tautological to a certain extent, paradoxical. It resembles the advertising market. Its contents are devoid of intention.

This theory may have quite a few arguments to back it, but I cannot help wondering: a) whether the stress has not been placed exclusively on the reverse or negative side of the system, which cannot be denied; b) how the emergence of this system can be explained, when one seems to be able to discern a certain continuity with the past. In my eyes, the present situation is an extension of the past one, even though it may try to pass itself off as a revolution. The two are not mutually exclusive; c) whether it is fair to leave out certain plasticians or artists who are no doubt more difficult to situate within this totalizing grid (Picasso, Dubuffet).

Now, Marcel Duchamp, according to certain commentators the launcher of Ready-Made art and therefore of this "wholly artificial product," went even further in the imposture. I have already referred to him as an "illusionist in the second degree." Let us return to the famous episode of the urinal: "The hanging committee (of the Society of Independent Artists) received something most embarrassing from a certain R. Mutt, of Philadelphia: a urinal which had been overturned, and conspicuously signed, dated, and entitled *Fountain*. The urinal was conjured away; at any rate, it does not appear in the catalogue. There was no public scandal. The exhibition was a great success, and it is only in May, at its closure, that in the second issue of the satirical review *The Blind Man*, an anonymous editorial entitled *The Richard Mutt case* appeared, which sided with R. Mutt's choice.[3]"

Marcel Duchamp's adversaries may gloat: his strategy—ensuring the success of the urinal (the *Fountain*)— fulfils the main requirements mentioned above (which explain the process of transition from an object void of meaning to the affirmation: "this is a work of art"), and at the same time, overcomes them. Indeed, the public never saw this famous fountain, since it was never exhibited (only later did it see the photograph taken, it is true, by Alfred Stieglitz, a friend of Duchamp).

This Ready-Made work, which went unnoticed, was aided by no scandal. Besides, in a declaration to the press, which was issued on the day following the opening (the author of this apparent hoax, Marcel Duchamp, was present), it was specified that it had been agreed unanimously by the auctioneers that "The (received) Fountain... is not a work of art, according to any definition whatsoever."

d) It is not the institution either which has contributed to raising its status, since it rejected the piece from the start.

In spite of this unique situation—whereby the rules designed to govern the fraudulent passage from the void object to the work of art were not applied—, it triumphed, as if the ban placed on the piece had been the best launching-pad it could have hoped for. Without having been totally aware of it himself, Marcel Duchamp devised a most efficient and cunning device: scandal—in this case censorship—was the best way to ensure a prestigious promotion of his work.

(3) — Thierry de Duve, *Résonances du ready-made*, Ed. Jacqueline Chambon, Nîmes, 1989, p. 46.

Negative interpretations are once again responsible for keeping protests and lamentations going.[4]

This revolutionary art, which makes use of harsh methods, even crazy ones, seems to be wholly negative, which is why it may be disappointing or shocking. Nonetheless, it has paved the way for modernity, which has responded with an irruption, as if it had suddenly been freed.

The *Fountain* was considered a godsend to be grasped in order to prove the fraudulence and insignificance of contemporary art, seemingly based on a swindle or on deception.

But one forgets that one proceeded with elimination in order to make way for the creation which was to follow. Besides, artists themselves have recognized in this joke the starting-point of a new adventure on which they are embarked. Ready-Made art was a turning point which forced one, in salutary fashion, to question things permanently.

***

Nowadays, art is in the hands of a few specialists who continue to hate their contemporaries. Even though our era is generally moving towards a lessening, if not the end of all exclusionist tendencies, there are gurus who intend to maintain the divisions and consequently defend the past. It seems that the only task the artist who applies himself to the world of utensils—to "domo-aesthetics"—has set himself is to deride and to profane everything: he is considered an "undoer" and a debaser.

These modern watchdogs appeal instead to metaphysical art, which, they maintain, reveals superior essences and the transcendant, or else to an art which delves into the dramas of the human soul in search of an ideal.

In their eyes, the act of "doing" is of lesser value than that of "being," as if the artist were now a grand priest of some religion, officiating in order to give thanks to a mystery, or, conversely, as if it were their role to condemn the artist who strays in the direction of some artificial paradise.

But this fairy tale is out of date: it flourished during the decadent

(4) — Thierry de Duve, op. cit., has been explicit on the matter. I do not share his negative viewpoint, because in my opinion, Ready-Made art has shaken the world and succeeded in evicting an art form which was already in the wane and which was becoming mannered. It would have died anyway, given the lack of renewal. Thanks to his extreme impertinence, Duchamp managed to put an end to it once and for all.

period of the Romantic era, and has worn out those who kept it going, as well as those who suffered from it.

Surely, the criteria on which one should rely and the factor which allows one to recognize real arrangements or structures (montage, or installation-works, to use the proper terms, which themselves derive from window-dressing and from promotional displays), in other words the genuine work of art, is the ability to stimulate and give life to numb or dulled senses.

It is to the body, and to its rich potentialities to which I commend myself, for it reacts to new things, whereas it gradually becomes numb in the presence of the same old things. It is necessary to shake it out of its apathy, to put forward an environment which will invigorate it. Early on, already, Valéry came up with a suggestive definition: "One should place in this category (in this art-form) those works which have no clearly defined or uniform physical role"—underline in the text. "Indeed, these are sensory modifications which are not indispensable to the human being, and as a whole, they constitute our greatest treasury, it is to them we owe our richness. It is these infinite resources which give rise to our wealth of art.[5]"

Consequently, let us stop separating our interior environment from our exterior one, the art gallery from the street and from the rest of the city!

Art must be seen to penetrate everything around us. It must be allowed to pull down the last partitions. This was my aim in paying so much attention to the intersection between the two opposing movements: art proper and design.

The first goes down to meet the object, or even the monument: it attemps to escape the flat surface in which it has been enclosed for so long. The second climbs out from the prosaic and humble object towards a morphology which is not reduced to mere utility.

Although unequal in strength, the two are combined: it is both the interest of art and that of the banal object to join up and to merge. The one will gain in consistency, whilst the other will lose, definitively, that which weighed down upon it and confined it to functionalism.

(5) — Valéry, *Œuvres complètes*, vol. 1, N.R.F., Paris, 1957, p. 1311.

INDEX

BIBLIOGRAPHY

Apollinaire (Guillaume), *Œuvres complètes*, "Les peintres cubiques"; edited by M. Décaudin, A. Balland et J. Lecat, Paris, 1966.

Aragon (Louis), *les Collages*, § La peinture au défi, Hermann, Collection Savoir, Paris, 1980.

Archipenko (Alexandre), *Manifeste de la polychromie, Œuvres*, Visionnaire International, 1969

Baudelaire (Charles), *Art in Paris 1845-1862. Salons and other Exhibitions reviewed by Charles Baudelaire*, translated and edited by Jonathan Mayne, Phaidon Press, London, 1965.

Bergson (Henri), *The Two Sources of Morality and Religion*, Henry Holt and Company, New York, 1935.

Boccioni, *Dynamisme plastique, peinture et sculpture futuristes,* L'Age d'Homme, Paris, 1975

Christo, Le packaging, *Dynasteurs*, octobre 1986

Claudel (Paul), *Œuvres en prose*, Bibliothèque de la Pléiade, Paris, 1965

Colin (Christine), *Philippe Starck*, Pierre Mardaga, Liège, 1989

Concepts of Modern Art, edited by Nikos Stangos, Thames and Hudson, London, reprinted 1990.

Coplans (John), Don Judd : An interview with John Coplans, in *Don Judd* (catalogue), Pasadena Art Museum, 1971

Dagognet (François), *Rematérialiser, la pensée de l'impensable,* Introduction au Catalogue de la Galerie Nationale du Jeu de Paume in Jean Dubuffet, les dernières années, 1991 - Santachiara ha glorificato la merce, in *Santachiara, L'estetica dell'uso*, Reggio Emilia, 1990

Dobrowolski (Zygmunt), *Etude sur la construction des systèmes de classification*, Gauthier Villars, 1964

Dubuffet (Jean), *l'Homme du commun à l'ouvrage*, Idées/Gallimard, Paris, 1973 - *Bâtons rompus*, Minuit, Paris,1986

Durkheim (Emile), *les Formes élémentaires de la vie religieuse.* PUF, Paris, 1979

Duve (Thierry de), *Résonnances du readymade*, Jacqueline Chambon, Paris, 1989

Giedion (Siegfried), *Mechanization Takes Command. A Contribution to Anonymous History*, W. W. Norton and Company, New York/London, 1969.

Gombrich (Ernst H.), *Art and Illusion,* Phaidon Press, Oxford, 1960.

Goulet-Cazé (Marie-Odile), *l'Ascèse cynique*, Vrin, Paris, 1986

Kémeny (Zoltan), entretien réalisé par Claude Gintz, in « Artistes », n°14, avril-mai 1980

Lambert (Jean-Clarence), *le Parti-pris des objets*, « Opus », avril 1969 Interview de juin 1976

Le Corbusier, *l'Art décoratif aujourd'hui*, Arthaud, coll. l'Esprit nouveau - *Vers une architecture*, G. Crès et Cie

Léger (Fernand), *Functions of Painting*, The Viking Press, New York, 1973.

Leiris (Michel), *Afrique Noire : la création plastique*, Gallimard, Paris, 1962

Leroy (Louis) , L'exposition des impressionnistes, in « Le Charivari », 1874

Marcuse (Herbert), *One-dimensional Man. Studies in the Ideology of Advanced Industrial Society*, Beacon Press, Boston, 1964.

Mauss (Marcel), *Sociologie et Anthropologie*, PUF, 5th ed., Paris, 1973

Plato, *The Laws*, translated by Trevor J. Saunders, Penguin Books, Harmondswoth, 1970.

Ponge (Francis), *Méthodes*, Idées/Gallimard, 1961 - *le Parti-pris des choses* - l'Ustensile, in *Le Grand Recueil, Méthodes*, Gallimard, NRF, Paris, 1949

Rey (Robert), *Contre l'art abstrait*, 1957

Rosenberg (Harold), *The De-definition of Art*, The University of Chicago Press, Chicago and London, 1983.

Sartre (Jean-Paul), *Situations III,* Gallimard, NRF, Paris, 1949

Schapiro (Meyer), "Avant-Garde. The Apples of Cézanne. An Essay on the Meaning of Still life", in *Selected Papers, Modern Art*, New York, 1977 – "The Still Life as a Personal Object — A Note on Heidegger and Van Gogh", in *The Reach of Mind*, New York, 1968.

Stella (Frank), entretien réalisé par Claude

Gintz, in « Artistes », n°14, avril-mai 1980

Tapiès (Antoni), *l'Art contre l'Esthétique*, Galilée, Paris, 1974

Tardieu (Suzanne), *le Mobilier rural et traditionnel français*, Aubier-Flammarion, Paris, 1976

Thom (René), *Apologie du Logos*, Hachette, Paris,1990

Valéry (Paul), « Fragments des mémoires d'un poème » in *Variétés*, tome 5, NRF, 1945 -*Œuvres* complètes, tome 1, NRF,Paris,1957

Vasarely, *Plasticité*, Casterman/poche, Paris, 1970

Venturi (Robert), *l'Ambiguïté en architecture,* Dunod, 1971

Wood (Walter A.),*Circular for the Year* (catalogue)

Zola (Emile), *l'Œuvre,* Gallimard,/Folio, 1983

CONTENTS

Achevé d'imprimer
par Mame Imprimeurs à Tours
Dépôt légal : Février 1993
N° 29620